Contents

Social Work in a Changing World Series

Introduction to the series
Since the end of the 1980s we have witnessed considerable political, economical, social and cultural change in eastern, western and central Europe.

The scope and depth of change have been particularly dramatic in the post-Communist countries, of which Russia is the biggest and the most influential.

These changes have confronted all of us who are interested in the well-being of the citizens of Europe with new, unprecedented challenges.

A number of new groups have become vulnerable in a way they were not before, while the old systems of welfare began to crumble and their inability to provide economic, social and psychological safety nets became manifested.

This has led to readiness to look for new ways of meeting the emerging needs of the population has been developing among policy makers, welfare workers and academics. Appetite for learning has been encouraged by visits from and to western Europe and the United States, by getting access to some of the experiences and literature available in the west on some of these issues.

At times such visits were all too short; the material looked at not particularly relevant; the cultural differences felt unbridgeable; and issues of power and hegemony too uncomfortable to confront.

Professional social work is one such main new way of responding to the new situation, its challenges, obstacles and opportunities.

While there were always people who helped others informally and formally, child care inspectors and social pedagogues who focused on children and recreational activities, professional social work did not exist in the Soviet Union, while some forms of it existed in Czechoslovakia, Romania and Slovenia.

The uniqueness of social work lies in the attempt to offer a personalised service which holds together the psycho-social levels of our existence by professionally qualified workers who also act as intermediaries between the service-user and the State. Usually social workers are not policy makers, though they may - and in my view should - attempt to influence policy decisions. Social workers are accountable to their employers, but their first and foremost loyalty is to defending vulnerable people in our society.

They do so in a variety of ways, which are based on knowledge of how people develop, interact, change, learn, become motivated, or despair; of how societies influence the lives of individuals; and of how to tread that fragile boundary between influence, coercion and enabling people to determine their choices and to put these into practice.

They are successful at times, unsuccessful at other times. Therefore the knowledge of the evaluative evidence on social work is crucial for improving its effectiveness, as well as for ensuring that newcomers to social work will learn from mistakes made in western social work, and will not need to repeat the mistakes, only to make their own, new mistakes.

An important component of social work is the belief that usually we do not know what is the best choice for another person; that s/he knows better than anyone else what is good for them, even when they need to know a lot more about alternative possibilities, the relative advantages and disadvantages of alternative courses of action, and even when they need to learn how to make decisions.

This belief contrasts sharply with the view of authoritarian regimes that they have the right to dictate to people what each of them should do individually, and with traditions of top-bottom advice giving and handing out benefits. To acquire the ability to encourage people in a crisis situation to express themselves, to weigh possibilities and to make decisions, to support them in implementing these decisions requires not only a non-authoritarian stance but also a genuine belief that all of us have the right and the ability to lead a reasonably satisfactory life, however varied the range must be.

Social work does not exist outside of specific political and cultural contexts. In the west it originated within the context of liberal capitalism. As liberal capitalism is now challenged by the New Right and pro-"free"-market orientation western social work finds itself in a serious crisis in terms of its adherence to values, conceptual and practice frameworks which come from a previous dominant ideology.

This fact must be baffling for east Europeans impressed by the richness of fabric of services and professional activities of western social work, to the point that they may see the notion of such a crisis as western indulgence.

Yet often westerners would not share with their eastern European friends their knowledge of this crisis, for fear that this may prevent the latter from being inter- ested in social work at all.

The position taken throughout the series SOCIAL WORK IN A CHANGING WORLD has been concerned with the wish to share our ideas about social work as honestly as possible, warts and all, crisis and disillusionment, in the belief that this is the best way for the development of social work, wherever it is taking place.

Therefore, the form which social work should take in any one country has to come out of the context of the specific country; imitation of models of social work used elsewhere is unlikely to work well without such an adaptation.

Yet this series is based on the belief that nevertheless the core of social work is international because it is based on common human experience, and to provide a guide to the content and format of social work in any one country (Midgely and Khinduka, 1992). That core consists first and foremost in social work values (Shardlow, 1989), including:

- the right of individuals to be supported by their communities and societies when facing adversity and becoming vulnerable;

- the right to be treated with respect and be offered dignity;

- the right to self-determination, as long as it does not entail risk to oneself and/or others;

- the right to fail and the right to fulfil one's potential constitute integral components of the right to self-determination.

- the responsibility of individuals for their own actions.

This is followed by the generalised knowledge of:

- how people develop and change;

- the role played by society in such a process;

- how they respond to adversity;

- what helps people in a crisis and what does not;

- what supports them in a way which enables them to take greater control over their reality and to use their potential.

The core skills which are based on the values and knowledge consist of:

- the ability to communicate with people experiencing adversity;
- the ability to form a good, personalised yet professional relationship with clients in which empathy and genuiness are expressed on the one hand and which is free from exploitation on the other;
- the ability to connect people to existing networks and create new networks if required;
- the ability to advocate and intermediate;
- knowledge and use of a wide range of formal and informal resources in the community;
- the ability to counsel individuals, families and groups;
- the ability to live with the losses and pain experienced by others without succumbing to the impact of such suffering oneself;
- the ability to reflect on and evaluate one's own work and change it in the light of the lessons thus learned.

Furthermore, it is productive to learn about how other societies go about their social work framework, as such learning generates ideas and helps to prevent the repetition of mistakes.

Reading about different approaches to social work is the least-coercive way to influencing people interested in learning about social work in post-Communist countries, for it allows them to reflect on what they have read, decide on their own what appeals to them and how to use it.

In social work we believe that reflection is indispensable in taking stock of situations and processes, of our own activities and those of others, and as a necessary, but insufficient condition for the provision of a personalised service (Schon. 1983).

Such a reflection is necessary for the navigation through the eternal dilemmas which social workers face constantly. For example, it would be naïve and misleading to suggest that social work is providing support only to people in adversity; it is also one of the more sophisticated tools of social control invented by liberal capitalism.

It exercises social control in a variety of ways, ranging from the coercive form of taking children away from their parents and recommending that people should be admitted to psychiatric hospitals to influencing people's views of themselves and others at the psychological level.

Indeed, the conflict between exercising care and control and the inevitability that care does not come without some type of control is one of the dilemmas which all social workers face in every society.

This dilemma relates to yet another problematic issue: namely, with whom does the primary loyalty of the social worker lie: is it with the State? with the specific employer? with the identified client? with the society in which the worker operates? In terms of our core values, this loyalty has to be first to the client, and then to society, with the loyalty to the employer and the State trailing behind. Such a commitment may be seriously tested at times, and social workers require considerable peer and professional support to stick by the loyalty to the client and to society in general.

A good text on any aspect of social work would need to pay attention to these dilemmas.

The new series is thus dedicated to the coverage of social work values, knowledge and skills, in the context of different needs, wishes, client groups, and social contexts.

It is not accidental that the series forms a part of the activities of the TRANS-FORMATION PROJECT OF THE HUMANITIES AND THE SOCIAL SCIENCES of the Soros Cultural Initiatives Foundation in Moscow. It was the initiative of Professor Teodor Shanin - the director of the project until November 1994 - to put social work on the map of the Transformation Project and its alliance with the Russian Ministry of Higher Education which have led to the beginning of the dialogue among British, American and Russian social work educators in the first place. The initiative has been supported systematically from its inception by the current director of the project, Mr. Victor Galizin.

In a number of ways, the move to develop professional social work in post-Communist countries embodies the challenges, opportunities and obstacles which we are confronted with throughout Europe, but in particular in post-Communist societies. Social work challenges traditional beliefs on the relationships between citizens and officialdom; the role of officialdom; the rights and responsibilities of individuals versus. the rights and duties of the State; the relationship between individuals and their communities; the abilities and potential of vulnerable people; the often fragile balance between the rational and the emotional compo-nents of our existence; care and control, and the nature of professionalism (Payne, 1991).

Thus it befits the Transformation Project, dedicated to introducing tools to facilitate transformation in the Humanities and the Social Sciences, to include the introduction of social work as a social science discipline as one of its core activities.

Professor Shulamit Ramon
series editor

References

Midgely, J; Khinduka, S; Hokenstad, M. (ed.) (1992) International Profiles of Social Work, American Social Workers Association, Washington.

Payne, M. (1991) Modern Social Work Theory: A Critical Introduction, Macmillan, London.

Schon, D. (1983) The Reflective Practitioner: How professionals think in action, Basic Books, New York.

Shardlow, S. (ed) (1989) The Value of Change in Social Work, Routledge, London.

Acknowledgements

I should like to thank the authors who agreed so readily to share their ideas. My special thanks go to Pauline Roberts, without whom this book would not exist.

Phyllida Parsloe

The authors

Margaret Boushel is a Lecturer in Social Work at Bristol University. For many years she was a social worker, manager and policy adviser on child care in local authority social service departments in England and Scotland. Her writing and research interests include cross-national approaches to child protection, social work with disadvantaged children and families and the strategies parents use to protect their children from abuse.

John Carpenter is a qualified social worker and a chartered psychologist. He is currently Senior Lecturer in Mental Health at the University of Kent at Canterbury, England. He practises family therapy with adults with mental health problems and their families. He is currently researching the effects of a project to involve and empower clients of mental health services and their families. He has co-edited two books on using family therapy in health and welfare services in Britain and is co-author of *Problems and Solutions in Marital and Family Therapy*. He is also joint editor of the *Journal of Family Therapy*.

Ram A. Cnaan is an Associate Professor at the University of Pennsylvania School of Social Work. He received both his BSW and MSW from the Hebrew University in Jerusalem, Israel, and his PhD in Social Work from the University of Pittsburgh. Dr. Cnaan's research focuses on volunteers in human services, voluntary action and organisations, community mental health, community organisation from an international perspective, religiously based social service delivery, and policy practice. Dr. Cnaan has published numerous articles in these areas and serves on the editorial board of seven journals. Recently, Dr. Cnaan was elected chairperson of the editorial board of *Nonprofit and Voluntary Sector Quarterly*. Currently, Dr. Cnaan serves as a Vice-President for Meetings of the Association of Researchers in Nonprofit Organisations and Voluntary Action (ARNOVA).

Elaine Farmer is a Lecturer and Research Fellow in the Department of Social Work at Bristol University. She practised as a social worker in the UK and Australia before joining the university. Her research includes a national study of the reunification of separated children with their families published as *Trials and Tribulations: Returning Children from Local Authority Care to their Families* and a study of the links between decision-making, intervention and outcome in child protection work in the UK which is published under the title *Child Protection Practice: Private Risks and Public Remedies* and co-authored with Morag Owen. Her current research is on residential and foster care for sexually abused children and young abusers.

Ludmila Harutunian is a Member of the Armenian National Academy of Philosophical Science; Deputy Chief of the Armenian Women's Council; formerly a member of the Soviet Parliament; Head of the Department of Sociology at Yerevan State University, Republic of Armenia. She has written three books and published sixty articles. Currently interested in establishing social work as a discipline within the Department of Sociology. Research interests includes responses to social transition, poverty and alternative economies, and women's responses to disasters.

Kwong Wai Man graduated from the University of Hong Kong with a Bachelor of Science degree in 1973 and a Master in Social Work in 1975. After his social work education, he started working at the Boys' and Girls' Clubs Association of Hong Kong. During the nine years he worked in this agency he was responsible for the development of a number of new services for young people, including out-reaching social work, school social work, and family life education service at various times. He was also responsible for the development of research work and staff training programmes of the agency. In 1980 he obtained one-year study leave to study for a MEd degree at the Ontario Institute for Studies in Education, majoring in counselling and adult education. He had developed a strong interest in the area of parent education and counselling at the time he left the agency in 1984. He entered social work teaching in that year at the then City Polytechnic of Hong Kong (now the City University of Hong Kong) and has been teaching in the area of social work theories and practice ever since. He is currently responsible for the development of field training for social work students. He has contributed conference papers and research papers on such topics as counselling and counsellor education, community care, dual-earner families child care, and parent education. He is currently working on two action research projects related to the field training of social work students. He is currently studying for his PhD degree at the University of Bristol. His PhD thesis is on the professional development and change of social workers.

Audrey Mullender is the Director of the Centre for Applied Social Studies at the University of Durham. She has sixteen years' experience of social work education, building on a background in social services and a continuing involvement in the voluntary sector. She is the author of over sixty social work publications and has taught and lectured in many countries around the world. Her current special interests include groupwork, domestic violence and adoption.

Phyllida Parsloe trained as a probation officer and then moved into psychiatric social work. She found a delight in teaching medical students and switched into social work education at the London School of Economics. After a spell teaching American law students how to interview she returned to Britain to establish a social work department at the University of Aberdeen in Scotland and later at the University of Bristol in England. The Bristol Social Work Department now has links with St. Petersburg University of Social Science and the Humanities.

Rose Rachman was formerly a lecturer at LSE - in social work theory and practice; health social work as an area of particular practice; Vice-Chair BASW specialist group in health-related social work; tutor for Open University, subject specialist assessor for HEFC. Formerly a Principal social worker in health service social work, Principal training officer, student unit supervisor, deputy manager of department in a voluntary organisation. Current research interests - community care and health-related social work; women and health; developing social work as a discipline in Armenia; developing a women's centre in Armenia as a response to a natural disaster. Recent articles on social work and discharge planning; community care and the changing role of social work; disasters and reflections on resilience.

Jill Reynolds is a lecturer in the School of Health and Social Welfare at the Open University. She has worked as a social worker, and as a trainer in work with refugees She has been a lecturer on social work qualifying courses. Her publications include (with Rosalind Finlay) *Social Work and Refugees* (1987), and co-editorship of *Health, Welfare and Practice: Reflecting on Roles and Relationships* (1993). She has also written on mental health and refugees, on learning how to work with interpreters, and on the teaching of gender issues in social work education. She is currently preparing open learning materials for a degree level course in mental health.

Olive Stevenson is Professor of Social Work Studies at the University of Nottingham in the UK. She has particular interests in the social care of very elderly people and in child welfare, on both of which she has undertaken research and published extensively. She is a member of the European Community Committee on Science & Technology for Elderly People (COST A5), in which 17 countries participate, and of the British Government's Social Security Advisory Committee.

Erika Varsanyi was born in Budapest, studied law and worked as a scientific assistant and took part in various sociological research projects; with a MA in sociological studies she worked as a sociologist in a psychiatric setting. Later she made extended studies in villages of group dynamic and the social history of mental illnesses. Her PhD is about the context of self-destructive tendencies based on this work. Since 1989 she has been teaching in the Department of Social Policy, at the University of Pecs

In the period of political transition she initiated programmes in several villages to establish civil organisations, especially in underprivileged regions and social groups (e.g. gypsy people and unskilled workers).

Introduction

This book is about ways in which people can increase their control over their own lives and over the kind of social services which government and the independent sector sponsor or provide and the ways in which services are offered. The current term being used for this process is empowerment and as the chapters which follow show, this is not a simple or uncontentious concept.

No definitive definition of empowerment is offered here because the concept is still evolving and it means different things to different people. It is used to refer to users of social services having greater control over the services they receive and here is concerned with the individual service level. It can also refer to a more general level of planning for services at the local, regional or national level when services users are involved in advising, and less frequently in deciding on the services to be provided. It may be seen as a way to reduce professional power or a ploy used cynically by professionals to protect their status and power. Its purpose may be to promote the personal growth of those empowered, to raise the quality and appropriateness of social services or to give the disadvantaged members of society some influence which may lead to their attaining greater political power.

Because of its several meanings and purposes, the authors of the chapters that follow were not given any brief about the nature of the empowerment which they were to address. Each was asked to give their own definition and this is what has been done. All, however, are concerned either with the empowerment of individuals or families in relation to the way they organise their own lives and the services they require or the empowerment of groups who need services for themselves at a local level. We do not deal here with issues of user involvement and empowerment at a wider regional or national, strategic or policy, level.

Empowerment in social work is a western concept originating probably in the United States but picked up quickly in Britain. As social work educators and practitioners from the West make contact with those who are developing social work and social services in the former Communist countries, the concept of empowerment spreads and this book itself is part of this process. Whatever the definition of empowerment, it necessarily involves an increase in the power of users of social services. The potential for such an increase and the form it can take will depend upon the cultural as well as the political and economic context. What is appropriate for one culture and system cannot be transplanted unchanged into another. The chapters in Part II are all to some extent concerned with the interplay of culture, politics, economy and empowerment.

Cnaan's chapter can be mistaken for a defence of residual welfare and/or a capitalist economy. On closer scrutiny, it can be seen that he is arguing that if the former Communist States are, for better or worse, to move to a capitalist economy they may need to develop some of those aspects of a civil society which the more fortunate parts of the United States enjoy. In his example, voluntary organisations like those organising children's football leagues, provide a means by which people who have little power or satisfaction at work can feel empowered through providing a needed service. Others, like Putnam, take this argument further, suggesting that such organisations constitute "social capital" and its presence or absence affects the quality of local government as well as economic prospects (Putnam 1993).

Varsanyi, too, is writing about civil engagement and the struggle to develop, or perhaps redevelop, social capital in Hungary. Some writers have suggested that during its period of independence between the two World Wars Hungary developed a tradition of voluntary work and non-government organisations (Hegeshi and Talygar in Khnikuda 1992). However, the gypsies with whom the author and her students were working would have been unlikely to have been part of or benefited from this experience since they were a particularly oppressed and marginal group.

The later chapter which comes into Part III about work with women in Armenia is also concerned with a society in transition to which the natural disaster of an earthquake has dealt an almost paralysing blow. As an aside, the authors comment upon the effect of western aid which encourages a culture of dependency in which people come to expect financial assistance almost as of right. On this world-wide scale, and in the more local scale of community or family work, we need to be aware of the complexities of the gift relationship. Loans, whether they be in kind or in service, demand repayment and without such reciprocity the receiver may be disempowered and one outcome is the creation of a culture of dependency.

Kwong Wai Man writes from Hong Kong, a city state which is still a colony of the United Kingdom and has probably one of the most successful capitalist economies in the world. In political terms it faces a change from British patriarchal paternalism to whatever Chinese rule may bring after 1997; and there is little certainty what this will mean. This chapter deals with the tendency of social work academics and practitioners to import concepts from other cultures into their own as if they can be culture free - which of course they cannot. This chapter raises the question of what empowerment does and will mean in a city like Hong Kong where Chinese and western cultures have mixed relatively freely for a long time and where citizens are facing the uncertainty of what the future will hold. It is somewhat surprising that in a society which is usually considered to have a particular respect for authority, be it that of ancestors, parents, teachers or governors, community action has had apparently so much success.

Part III is concerned with the pathways to empowerment for particular groups of people who are disadvantaged in modern societies: women, older people and refugees. It did not prove possible, although it would have been appropriate, to include discussion of social work with people with mental and physical disability and with members of racial minorities, although in the chapter in Part II Varsanyi does deal with gypsies who are a racial minority.

The three chapters in this part illustrate clearly how pathways to empowerment will differ to take account of the particular strengths and needs of any individual or group. One way to help the women of Gymri to gain some sense of control over their lives was to encourage the traditional craft work which had been a feature of women's life in Armenia. In some ways this might seem to be at odds with a wish to empower and then perhaps to liberate women from their traditional roles. The authors decided, and probably quite correctly, that the most important thing to do was to find something which was likely to succeed so that these women, shattered by almost unimaginable loss and grief, could find some chink of hope for the future. Moving out from traditional roles could come later.

For elderly people, Stevenson suggests that the small particulars of life may be an area over which they can be empowered to have control. This is an important point for social workers who may feel they have no power to influence the major decisions in social policy and ignore the small choices which users can make if these are recognised as important and freed from bureaucratic control.

Reynolds recognises the small steps which can be taken with refugees who are separated by culture and language from the community in which they settle. She also makes the very important point that those who seek to empower users may find themselves trying also to empower the social welfare staff who are responsible for providing services to marginalised groups. Social workers often assume that someone somewhere, and usually at a distance up the hierarchy, has power and needs to be forced to use it on behalf of those who are disadvantaged. There may be some truth in this view but it also seems to be a feature of power distribution, at least in a democratic society, that everyone thinks that the power lies with someone else. If one accepts Foucault's view of the distribution of power then this is right. Power is actually diffused through society. One of the skills for those whose aim is to empower others is to enable those they work with to recognise the power they hold. As a social work teacher, I am frequently surprised that students see themselves as powerless and oppressed whereas in many ways I experience them as a powerful influence or barrier upon what I can do. The same is true of users and social workers and front-line social service staff and their managers.

The other issue, which this point raises but which is also apparent throughout the volume, is that empowerment is in large part a matter of attitudes: those of the user and those of the worker. People cannot move directly from oppression to empowerment; there are particular pathways for each individual, group or community and the skill of the social worker is to help them choose the most accessible route for themselves. To do this they may first have to change their attitude towards themselves so that they no longer, like the Armenian women, feel like a fly in a bottle.

Perhaps even more important are the attitudes of social workers, something which is stressed throughout this book. Front line staff in social services are being asked to empower users and yet their managers have not started to provide an example and an experience of empowerment of staff for these workers to draw upon in their work with users. I have argued elsewhere (Parsloe and Stevenson 1993) that if users are to be empowered the whole policy of social service agencies will need to change because most staff will find it difficult to empower users if they are not themselves empowered by their managers.

Even if empowerment becomes an agency-wide policy it will not be easy for managers or for workers. All have grown up in a society which tends to see helping as doing things for other people and knowing what is best for them. Seldom is it seen as assisting people to do what they want and in the ways they choose to achieve their aims. To recognise this is the first essential step since one of the major barriers is what Marsh and Fisher (1992) call the DATA effect; the "we do all that already" response. They were writing about a project which aimed to work in partnership with users and where staff were supposedly committed to this aim. Yet despite the evidence that they did not hear what users said, and that they imposed their preferences for outcome and process upon users, they still maintained that they already worked in partnership.

It may be useful to draw attention to two other important issues arising from Part II. The first is the potential conflict between the needs of one person in a group or a family for empowerment when it seems that an increase in their power will decrease the power of another person. This may seem to arise in families as Boushel and Farmer show as does Stevenson, and, in a later section, Carpenter. Increasing the power of older people may seem to decrease that exercised by their sons and daughters; empowering children may weaken the power of parents or vice versa, and sometimes empowered mothers could feel as if they are disempowered as women. Sometimes these perceptions of changes in power are real; some parents and some children, be they adults or juveniles, may hold more than an appropriate amount of power over others in the family and some adjustment may be needed. More often, perhaps, the empowerment of one person in a group or family is not at the expense of another and may, in fact, result in more freedom for the other person. The skill of the social worker lies in finding solutions which achieve something for all parties but this may not always be possible. Sometimes the needs of one person in a family are in conflict with those of another.

The second point made in these chapters is that empowerment cannot always be the primary goal of social work action. Sometimes children, old people, sick people and those who are mentally disabled actually need protection. The social worker will try to act in ways which provide the necessary protection and empower the individuals, or, in the case of a young child, the parents, to have as much control of their own lives as possible. But the first imperative may be to minimise risk.

The third part of the book looks at some of the social work methods which can be used to enable people to acquire greater power over their own lives. Here more forcefully than elsewhere, although it is always an issue, the writers are faced with the problem of how to avoid didactic writing about what has to be an enabling process. The writers here struggle, with more or less success, to avoid being prescriptive but do not always succeed, although they would, I think, agree that workers cannot learn to practise towards empowerment any more than users can become empowered by being told what to do. They need to change their own attitudes and develop their own facilitative styles of practice. But, as the sentence you have just read shows, it is difficult to write in facilitating language.

Underlying these chapters about methods is an unspoken assumption about a particular kind of professional which is in many ways the opposite of the traditional professional who is emotionally detached, has access to specialist expert knowledge unavailable to lay people and who directs the patient or client. If clients are to empower themselves they need a professional who is equally skilled but who behaves very differently. The professional who can best help others to empower themselves is a facilitator rather than expert, who tries, in the language of family therapy, to join or engage with users by getting alongside their feelings and who tries to share the knowledge they have so that the client can use it for his or her own ends. Both kinds of professionals need knowledge and skills but the professionalism of the enabling professional consists in their ability to help others to develop or restore their feelings of self-esteem and self-confidence so that they may empower themselves.

For some existing social workers and some students this enabling kind of professionalism runs counter to their perhaps unconscious wish to help through their greater knowledge and expert status. To work in this way means for them to lose power and some of the satisfaction in the job which lies in being in control. Those who achieve empowering practice would, however, argue that they gain rather than lose personally from giving up the role of expert of substantive knowledge and that it is both a privilege and self-fulfilling to assist others to empower themselves. Some social workers and students seem to have a natural bent towards empowering practice but may need the example and support of facilitative management and an appropriate style of education. Some of the educational issues are addressed in the final part of the book.

References

Fisher, M. and Marsh P. (1992) *Good Intentions* Joseph Rowntree Foundation. York.

Hegeshi and Talygar (1992) in Khnikuda, S. (ed) *Profiles of International Social Work*. American Association of Social Workers.

Parsloe, P. and Stevenson, O. (1993) *Community Care and Empowerment*. Joseph Rowntree Foundation. York.

Putnam, R. (1993) Making Democracy Work: Civic Traditions in Modern Italy. Princeton University Press.

Empowerment in Social Work Practice

Phyllida Parsloe

Summary

Social work has incorporated within its philosophy the idea of power-sharing with clients. The words used to describe this and the justifications for it have changed over time. These changes are explored as are the meanings attributed to its current expression in the word "empowerment."

Empowerment is a word which entered social work writing and thinking during the late 1980s and early 1990s but it represents a strand of thought with a much longer history. The particular words have changed but the underlying tensions which give rise to these ideas are not new and remain unchanged. These are the tensions between independence and dependency, autonomy and protection and citizens' rights and the power of governments.

Earlier attempts to manage these apparently contradictory conditions found expression in the years after the Second World War in the idea that social work existed to help people to help themselves, that clients had a right to self-determination, bounded only by similar rights in others and that the challenge for the social worker was to start where the client is, and to move at the client's pace. This somewhat muted approach to clients' rights matched a time in Britain when the newly created Welfare State was thought to have eliminated poverty and when the power imbalance between the providers of social services and those who were their recipients was not as fully recognised as it later came to be.

The main reasons for helping people to help themselves and the later versions of this same approach are threefold. There are ethical reasons, political reasons and psychological reasons. At different periods of time one of these reasons is likely to have been more stressed than others. Ethical reasons lie in beliefs about the proper way in which one human being should approach another, and these go back to beliefs about the intrinsic value of each person. They derive from Judeo-Christian thought but have been largely divorced from their religious roots and have become part of the rhetoric, if not the reality, of western society in the twentieth century.

Democratic beliefs provide the political reasons why power should be shared and why citizens should have a say in the way in which they are governed. Hallett points out (1987) that these ideas "stem from a concern with the sources and legitimacy of those in power and the relationship of citizens to those who govern".

This is a reason which can be called in aid, not just by citizen groups but also by one part of government in attempts to limit the power, either of another part of the government structure, or of professional groups. In Britain the need to transfer power to citizens has been used by central government in its attempts to restrict the powers of local government and also of professional groups such as teachers and social workers.

The third set of reasons are psychological. It is widely accepted that people are more likely to change or to follow through on actions and plans if they themselves have had a major part in both deciding that they want to change either themselves or their environment, and then in deciding how these changes are to be brought about. Motivation is an important issue in social policy because most services, either material or interpersonal, can only be successful if the recipient takes an active part. The best services and the most skilled counselling will be ineffective if the person receiving them has not been involved in the plans for them and does not want them. Stories abound in social work about elderly people who feed their meals-on-wheels to their pets; it is not they who should be criticised but the providers who either inflicted an unwanted service on the recipient or else failed to realise that the well-being of the loved cat or dog was of more importance to the elderly person than their own condition.

Linked to this psychological reason are the practical ones. Recipients are experts on the services they receive and are in the best position to give feedback to providers about what works and what does not. Inevitably, social policy which is enacted at a general level has to be adapted to the particular needs of many different individual recipients. This adaptation is what transforms what could be a bureaucratic, rule-bound service into a social work service. Such transformations can only take place when planning and implementation are the shared concern of recipient and provider.

The early post-war period placed most stress on the psychological reasons for client self-determination. This fitted the then most widely expressed view that the causes of persisting social problems lay in the pathology of individuals and families rather than in structural inequalities in society.

The next expression of this trend, which is currently expressed through notions of empowerment, came with the development of large social service organisations which had control over resources which many people wanted, such as day care for children or residential places for elderly people. They also had the power to initiate action which could result in the courts removing children from their parents. During the 1970s increasing attention began to be paid to the role citizens could and should play in local government and service delivery. This was not just a British phenomenon but can be seen in the "war on poverty" in the United States, the emphasis upon citizens' rights in Scandinavian welfare provision and in the Australian assistance plan of 1973. This was a period when social provision was multiplying and with it the discretion of the front-line staff who administer the services. An emphasis upon citizen participation was seen as one way to check this discretion which had become the object of attack in government and research reports.

The word used in the early 1970s was participation which, like several of the other words used to express the ideas we are considering, had the benefit of being capable of meaning many different things to different people. As Rose wrote in 1975:

"The problem with participation is that it is so ambiguous; each is free like Alice's Humpty Dumpty to make the word mean exactly what he or she wishes it to mean. Thus each - defining the concept suitably - is able to construe participation as synonymous with virtue."

There were, however, attempts to define the concept, one of the best known being Arnstein's eight-runged ladder of citizen participation (1972).

8	Citizen control	
7	Delegated power	Degrees of citizen power
6	Partnership	

5	Placation	
		Degrees of tokenism
4	Consultation	

3	Informing	
2	Therapy	Non-participation
1	Manipulation	

The idea of participation came in for some negative criticisms and since these criticisms can apply to empowerment also they are worth considering. Coit (1978) argued that participation was essentially conservative and tended to reinforce the *status quo*. Five reasons were given for this assertion:

> It tends to eliminate the notion of antagonism between the working and ruling classes.
>
> It encourages compromise and conciliation in order to obtain minimal concessions.
>
> It can be used to divert trouble-makers into less radical alternatives.
>
> It is individualistic and hinders collective approaches.
>
> It skims off local leadership.

These reasons suggest that employees of the State who attempt to involve clients in decisions are doing so for the wrong reasons. They have no intention of engaging in power-sharing, which is the intention behind participation, partnerships or empowerment, but rather are finding alternative means of manipulating clients.

While this may sometimes be the case a less-conspiratorial view might be to recognise that all these moves can easily be corrupted just because they are essentially about power-sharing. Few people relish giving up power, no matter how much they support ideologies of sharing. As social workers who embark on this pathway know, to share is to struggle.

Participation slid easily into ideas of partnership between clients and social workers. Partnership between parents and social services was embodied in the important 1989 Children Act which, for the first time, codified the legislation relating to child care in England and Wales. But this concept is, if anything, more difficult to define than is participation although a great deal of work has gone into attempts to clarify it and in particular to be clear about the amount of power or control which a client partner might expect to exercise.

A British voluntary organisation, the National Children's Bureau, mounted a project on "Parents in Partnership - Services for Families with Young Children" and the papers emerging from this had an important influence on the debate in Britain. Drawing on this work Pugh (1985 and 1987) attempted to develop a hierarchy of control and to locate partnership in it.

- Non-participation
- Being there
- Co-operation

- Collaboration
- Partnership
- Control

During the 1980s, and alongside partnership and participation, ideas drawn from the market economy began to infiltrate social policy and to influence social workers. Clients began to be referred to as customers and by implication were endowed with the power of choice which money provides to consumers of material products. Social workers by and large have rejected this approach and the majority would probably agree with Jones (a Director of Social Services) and Jowell (1987) when they wrote:

> "Social services are not based upon market forces but on a complex combination of political mandate, professional judgement and statutory requirement."

This is an important distinction and one that social workers, and especially social work managers, need to keep in mind. There are aspects of the market economy which are attractive to hard-pressed managers squeezed between the needs of their many, often poor and disabled, clients and the constant requirement from central government to cut costs. Efficiency and effectiveness are important considerations and so is value for money, provided it is not taken to mean that the cheapest service gives the greatest value. But these ideas can be implemented without falling for the patently absurd notion that, for example, those who cannot get to bed without assistance are, as consumers of a care service, in a position comparable to that of someone deciding which washing powder or even which washing machine to buy.

So the notion of clients as consumers has not taken hold in social work but perhaps instead the concept of empowerment has arrived. It seems to have developed about the same time in the late 1980s in the United States and Britain. In Britain, like partnership before it, it is a notion built into legislation. The guidance (1991) for the Community Care Act states:

> *The rationale for this reorganisation is the empowerment of users and carers. Instead of users and carers being subordinate to the wishes of service providers, the roles will be progressively adjusted. In this way, users and carers will be enabled to exercise the same power as consumers of other services. This redressing of the balance of power is the best guarantee of a continuing improvement in the quality of service.*

Department of Health 1991

This attempt to redress the power imbalance has several roots and appeals to a range of different audiences who more often find themselves in opposition rather than accord. The power that is to be restored to users is that of local authority social services agencies and their front-line professional social work staff. Their power is to be reduced and this is certainly part of the agenda of central government. But most professionals would also, at least theoretically, support this move for ethical and psychological reasons even if they have difficulty in adjusting their own behaviour to correspond with their philosophy.

What exactly does empowerment mean? It is a most unfortunate word for social work to have adopted because it can well be argued that the very idea that one person, a social worker, can empower another, a client, runs counter to the whole idea of greater equality of power on which the concept supposedly depends. Giving power implies that it is something in the gift of the social worker which can be withheld or withdrawn; this is far removed from ideas of clients' rights which they, the clients, hold, irrespective of the actions of the social worker. Rights may be ignored or overidden but cannot be extinguished whereas power that is given can be.

But the idea of empowerment cannot be dismissed so cynically and in any case as Gomm suggests it is a word which is likely to remain, however ill-defined it is:

> *In health, welfare and education services "empowerment" is a buzz word. It litters mission statements. It is a rallying cry for health and welfare charities. The time of empowerment has come and the word has taken its place among other descriptors of good things, such as "natural", "additive free", "community", "freedom", "quality", "truth" and "justice".*

> *What can we do with a term which on the right of politics can mean privatising public services, and on the far left can mean abolishing private services; which can mean all things to all men, and something different again to some women? In a rational world it would make sense to wipe the slate clean and start again, with this and other words which impede clear thinking. If what it designates has any merit, we should use other words instead.*

> *However, no one is going to give up using such a nice word for the time being and no one has the power to make them.*

He goes on to outline four ways of looking at the power relationship between health welfare and education services and users, suggesting it is possible to view this as:

an oppressive relationship which allows the powerful and/or rich to go on exploiting the powerless or poor. Those exploited may be the working classes, women or minority groups. Workers in these systems are oppressed, too, although they do not recognise this because they have been duped by the system;

a helping relationship in which workers assist users in ways they could not undertake alone. Workers have the expertise and may claim to know better than recipients what is good for them;

a disabling relationship in which workers and agencies exploit users for their own ends;

a brokerage relationship in which workers are seen as brokers between users and services.

These different views, as to the nature and use of power in service-user relationships, lead on to different meanings for empowerment. Where the relationship is exploitative, empowerment must consist in convincing the oppressed of their oppression in the hope that they will then band together to take hold of power. Workers stand side by side with users to contest the power of capital, racism or patriarchy. Some social group work has a component of this approach although in social work it is seldom taken to its logical conclusions. As Gomm points out, in Britain at least, few users are easily convinced that they are "dupes of a corrupt and oppressive system".

Where the relationship is seen as helping, power is not an issue. Empowerment means helping people who are at a personal or social disadvantage deal with their situation so that they have as good a chance as anyone else of taking advantage of opportunities. Clients may have increased confidence but Gomm suggests it is misleading to refer to this as empowerment.

Where power is disabling, the aim must be to make professionals and agencies responsive and accountable to users. Self-help groups are in part based upon this view of power and many social workers have contributed to establishing such groups and then withdrawing from them. Much of the central government thrust in Britain in recent years has been to make services more responsive to users.

Gomm suggests that brokerage requires that users have a more competitive edge in obtaining services. Here empowerment may mean "establishing and servicing lobby groups - running consultation exercises - and marketing positive images of previously stigmatised client groups". The best example in Britain is probably the way in which people with learning difficulties have acquired a new, more positive image, including a change of name from the former one of mental handicap, and have developed extensive advocacy and self-advocacy arrangements.

When social workers speak of empowerment they have seldom analysed the concept in the way Gomm has done. What they usually have in mind is a wish to assist or encourage clients to develop the confidence, competence and self-esteem to allow them:

- to have a greater say in services for themselves and their families
- to have a greater say, usually as part of a representative group, in the planning of services
- to join with others to create the services they want

In the chapters which follow, each of these types of empowerment is explored.

To state that clients should be enabled to have a greater say in service planning and provision needs further exploration. Clients need power over three aspects of services: the system from within which services are offered; the way in which services are provided; and the nature of the services themselves.

Britain has recently moved to what is now called pluralistic welfare provision; some services are now provided by the private sector, the voluntary sector and the statutory sector. One form of empowerment would be to enable clients and citizens who are involved on the individual level, in the planning of services for themselves, or on the collective level in planning them for a locality, to influence the mix between sectors. It may be a matter of great importance or complete indifference to a client whether the service they want, for example home care assistance to do essential shopping, is provided by a local firm which sells its services to the local authority, by a voluntary organisation who may be using volunteer helpers, or by the local authority social services department staff. Some clients feel strongly that they are entitled to such services and that they should be provided by the government. Others prefer a voluntary organisation and yet others may be more comfortable knowing that the service is purchased for them. Life-long political and ideological views will influence the choice a client makes. Similar views will be held by clients who share in local authority planning.

For many people the way in which a service is provided may be almost as important as the service itself. A meal delivered by a short-tempered person and at the wrong time may make it inedible, however hungry the recipient may have felt earlier. Because social services are largely personal, each person who receives them will have their own pattern of daily life into which the service must fit. Understanding these small particulars is an essential part of any power-sharing between social worker and client.

Finally, clients need a share in what services are provided individually and in a locality. Professionals sometimes fear that to enable clients to have power and choice will open the floodgates and overwhelm them with demands they cannot meet. Given the limited resources of social service agencies some staff believe that to offer such choice is akin to a confidence trick, since having elicited demands they would then be unable to meet them and clients would end up feeling more disempowered than they were before being asked. In fact research suggests that this is not the case and that the majority of clients are both restrained and realistic in assessing their own needs. In addition, they are also likely to ask for services which may be very different from those which the professionals think they need (Baldock and Ungerson 1994).

So far this discussion may have made power-sharing sound self-evidently right and something which social workers can and should embark on with all clients. However, social workers have other important responsibilities which are explored, particularly by Olive Stevenson and Margaret Boushel and Elaine Farmer (this book) in their chapters on work with older people and families where a child may be at risk. Sharing power should always be an aim in good social work but the degree to which it is possible must be tempered by issues of risk and the need for control. These raise difficult questions but they are ones which social workers must address and which they may, in many cases, be able to discuss openly with their clients, preferably together, but failing this on his or her own. A social worker may properly decide that in a particular situation at a specific point in time, protection and control are more important than power-sharing.

However, empowerment may be avoided for less appropriate reasons. Research (Marsh and Fisher 1992) suggest that social worker attitudes and habitual ways of behaving may get in the way. In Britain this has been recognised, particularly in relation to clients from minority groups or those who are old or have a disability. This tendency in social workers is explored in a later chapter.

Flawed as it may be, the thread of power-sharing which has run through social work is of fundamental importance if social workers are to put into practice the value they place upon each individual and the accountability they owe to their clients.

References

Arnstein, R. A. (1972). "Power to the People" *Public Administration Review*. Vol. 32.

Baldock, J. and Ungerson, C. (1994). *Becoming Consumers of Community Care*. Joseph Rowntree Foundation. York.

Coit, K. (1978). "Local Action not Citizen Participation" in Tabb, W. and Sawyers, L. *Marxism and the Metropolis*. New York. Oxford.

Department of Health. (1991). *"Practitioners and Managers Guide to Care Management and Assessment'"*. Her Majesty's Stationery Office. London.

Gomm, R. (1993) "Issues of power in health and welfare" in Walmsley, J; Reynolds, J; Shakespeare, P. and Woolfe, R. (eds.) *Health, Welfare and Practice: Reflecting on Roles and Relationships*. London: Sage.

Hallett, C. (1987). *Critical Issues in Participation*. Association of Community Workers. Newcastle upon Tyne. England.

Jones, A. and Howell, T. (1987). "May the Force be with you". *Insight*

Pugh, G. *et al.* (1987). *Partnership in Action*. Vols. 1 & 2. National Children's Bureau. London.

Rose, H. (1975). "The Icing on the Welfare Cake" in Jones, K. (ed.) *Yearbook of Social Policy*. Routledge and Kegan Paul.

Part I
Pathways through political contexts

Empowerment in a Period of Economic and Political Transition

Erika Varsanyi

Summary

This chapter focuses on community development in a period of political and economic transition in Hungary. It demonstrates, through three case studies, that the historical background can limit the opportunities to create autonomous local communities.

The process of transition was directed by intellectuals through negotiations with representatives of the former power. Therefore the majority of the society was not involved in this experience. The most marginalised groups of society suffer in the social crisis but they have no resources to solve their problems.

The projects focused on the empowerment of people living in different outlying areas in south-west Hungary. They were helped to organise themselves - with limited success - to obtain resources and to be independent of the State institutions. The help was offered by the author, a sociologist who developed skills in community work with gypsies and also engaged her own students in the project so that they could understand both theoretically and practically the opportunities and problems of empowerment. The critical question is how to empower both democratic representatives and, at the same time, civil organisations outside of the political institutions.

The concept of political participation involves the insertion of the various interests of citizens into the decision-making process. It takes for granted the organised presence of different interest groups, open decision making and the transfer of power through political processes. These are features which distinguish democracy as a political system from its opposite extreme of dictatorship.

The concept of civil society is of a community which organises itself to defend its negative freedom (Berlin 1990), to be independent from the State and not directed and controlled by the State. The organisations which defend the community from the intervention of the State lie outside political institutions and are formed by people with common interests. Political parties enforce ideas and interests within the framework of representative democracy. Civil organisations have to control and influence their own activities and hold together people with a community of interests (Pateman 1970). The societies of eastern Europe have much experience of dictatorship but lack experience of the democratic processes. Living within a dictatorship formed part of the socialisation of each individual. Generations of people learnt how to adapt to the political situation, how to behave as if they were not present and to live everyday life without the experience of a political existence.

The main difference between the histories of eastern and western countries can be seen in the relationships between local and centralised power. While the western countries developed from grassroots politics and became free from centralised power, the eastern countries suffered from a lack of local autonomy.

Social development in central Europe was affected by both processes. Until the sixteenth century the relationship between local and centralised power paralleled the western pattern. The occupation by the Ottoman Empire changed the situation to one of despotism (Szücs 1983).

Generations grew up accepting this framework of everyday life. The people behaved as if the framework were naturally given even if they did not always accept the lack of freedom. The horizons of life were set by the available knowledge which was defined by the power structure (Berger and Luckmann 1984).

The omnipotence of state power lead to the infantilisation of society. A dependence on state institutions generated fear and the majority of people in society relied for their existence on the State as the source of security. In this way the people became deprived of the capacity to deal with the issues which affected them. Certain groups were supported by the State, but rivalry between groups destroyed what little cohesion there was and the covert competition for support undermined any solidarity. The gradual softening of despotism provided the opportunity for independence in private life but the people did not learn how to live as citizens.

The brutal centralisation of state institutions deprived the local communities of the capacity for insight into the decision-making process.

We cannot speak about participation in those situations where the essence of the political system is the exclusion of the whole society from these processes. Hungarian society arrived at a crisis point in 1989.

In public life, associations, free trade unions and political parties were created but the unskilled people, who had been deprived of the capacity to develop their own opinions, were not included in these developments. They were not involved in the process of transition. The effects of this are reflected in the current dilemmas of civil society and exclusion of a representative democracy. People react to the new political system with fear and with aggressive distrust. The rate of participation in the first democratic election was not as high as would have been expected.

All hope disappeared when the first right-wing government was elected recently. The government did not show any sensitivity to the needs of the people and set limits on the freedom of the Press. The increase in unemployment shocked people who had always relied on state institutions for their security. Furthermore, because the former socialist regime had used the term "democracy" to describe itself, the idea was suspect when put forward as a characteristic of the new regime.

The style of the new government justified the traditional distrust. New governmental structures were established and local authorities in the villages were deprived of their institutional base. The people elected as local representatives in villages those who had played some role in public life or were recommended by others; some were elected almost by chance, because there were no local party organisations. Many of the more-skilled and educated families, who had some resources, had left the villages some years ago. The people who stayed presented a relatively homogeneous picture: unskilled labourers employed in low-paid state agriculture or industry. The local communities are also polarised along ethnic lines, in their ways of farming and in their loyalty to the former political system. The elected people come mostly from this labouring population but some of them had started to work as independent entrepreneurs.

The incompetence of local government became more obvious as social problems increased. The local communities were confronted with hopelessness compounded by unemployment. Without any financial resources or qualifications the people hoped for assistance from the local government or from somebody somewhere.

The local communities were locked into a traditional passivity, but social problems started to be addressed by non-governmental organisations. Associations and foundations were established, mostly by those who had more-secure life situations. The new market system economy provided the opportunity for those who had some resources to develop entrepreneurial activities, but for many people, living in small, poor, nearly empty villages, the market system offered only the hope of employment. But this hope is not realised either: the small enterprises in these villages only lasted a short time; the underdeveloped infrastructure made these areas unattractive to investors.

The dissatisfaction with the activity of local government created opportunities for individuals who showed special ability to organise and to represent the interests of the communities (Dewey 1992).

Empowerment came from the acknowledgement of their own capacities, which is a pre-condition for active participation as citizens. To be independent of the local and economic power did not happen without conflict. Although there were some associations which tried to function as political organisations by, for example, putting up a candidate for mayor, the persuasive distrust of parties and parliament deterred most from such a move.

The idea of civil society may seem to be controversial in this period of political-economic transition: on the one hand the civil organisations assist the integration of the community, the consciousness of civil presence; but on the other hand they increase alienation from political institutions.

The tensions between political institutions and society which has to organise itself could be resolved if we were able to accept this dichotomy (de Tocqueville 1983).

The following case studies illustrate the difficulties in empowering citizens to create structures of civil society. The first two describe the same community at two points in time, the third a different community.

1. The Romany Settlement: 1989 Fear and lack of capacity

The Romanies are the largest minority group in Hungary. They do not constitute a homogeneous group but include three main subgroups: (1) the Hungarian, the most integrated; (2) the most traditional subgroup, which speaks the Gypsy/Lovari language, mostly separated from the majority and traditionally dealing in commerce; (3) the group of Beas Gypsies who came in the last third of the nine-teenth century from Romania and who speak a Romanian-Hungarian mixed language.

It is the last group which is most prevalent in the south-west region of Hungary where I am working on these projects. They settled a century ago in Hungary, first outside the villages, in the forests. Later they moved closer to the villages to work for farmers. After the Communist regime was established the gypsies were forced into the unskilled labour market to work in industry and agriculture, like the farmers who were deprived of their land. Early in the 1960s, the Communist Party defined the traditional culture of the gypsies and their way of life as constituting social problems and ignored the unique characteristics of this minority. They ordered that these "problems" be treated by the state institutions. The tools of treatment used were welfare support, the building of new settlements by the State and education of gypsy children in special schools for the handicapped.

A lack of sophistication, reduced self-esteem and dependency made the Romany people unable to evaluate their situation effectively. Although satsfied with the basic security provided by the State, in the last five - six years it has been possible for different ethnic identities to re-emerge. The gypsy subgroups have formed their own associations and parties, but they still need the social security provided by the State.

I discovered a settlement of Beas-Romas along a road outside a village near the forest. The settlement consisted of 12 small houses. The forest was the place where the people had lived originally. Later, in order to work sometimes occasionally but sometimes more regularly, they moved closer to the village. Some years later they had to leave their site because floods destroyed their houses. They had nowhere to go. The magistrate solved the problem in a paternalistic way: he divided the land which belonged to the State into equal parts. However, this action had no legal basis. The houses which the people built by hand had no real authorisation. The settlement was technically illegal.

The current situation can be illuminated by asking the following questions:

- Could we identify a problem common to the members of this community?
- What kind of social tool did they use to solve it?
- What direction are they taking now?

The young generations pressed their claim for more-civilised housing but achieving this is hampered by the illegal situation. The process from total helplessness to empowerment starts when a problem is defined by the group itself. The goal of empowerment is to create a group which would be able to solve its problems itself. However, the conflicts inside this group made it impossible to move beyond their passivity and inertia. They could not change the situation in which they constantly insulted each other. The lack of representation and of information and the absence of problem-solving techniques aggravated the situation further. Doubts about ethnic identity were expressed in difficulties of adjusting to the majority but also in withdrawal from their own group.

We could not achieve a common problem resolution with this background. The local bureaucrats felt the effects of the political instability. Under pressure from the media, they sought to change the legal status of the settlement. It was not a result of common action but of my individual intervention. The legalisation offered the opportunity to build a house for one family only. The inhabitants did not really accept the process of political transition. They did not participate in the first election of 1990.

The members of the newly established local government tended to deny the social problems which had accumulated in the settlement. Increasing poverty has ended all hope of living in improved circumstances.

2. The Romany Settlement: 1989-1992

The road where the gypsies live leads to a little settlement. Originally it had been built both for the lessee of the large estate and for the families who lived and worked here. Collectivisation in 1948 brought little change to the lives of the families: they continued with agricultural work, although some of their experiences differed in the two periods. They remembered the private large estate structure as a patriarchal system, but collectivisation is remembered as an impersonal bureaucratic power.

Because of the subsequent lack of local agriculture, the gradual centralisation of life in the settlement has disintegrated and has become a lifeless place on the periphery. The socialist state agricultural factory dispossessed the uneducated people who had only agricultural skills. The fields, the agricultural building and also the inhabitants were in the hands of the agricultural factory.

When I went to that settlement in 1989 I found a confused situation centred on the destruction of the agricultural buildings. Forty families lived there mostly in wet, dark flats without any conveniences, even toilets. They did not own any property. Their collective memory has kept this experience as an incurable open wound: their request for the empty agriculture buildings from the management of the state factory was in vain. They were refused permission to use either the land for farming or the use of building materials.

This situation led me to look for activities and acceptable work for the people living there. When I gave a more focused direction to the group discussion and mentioned the opportunity for private farming separate from the state factory the people still employed quickly recognised the possible conflicts. They did not want to precipitate a confrontation and in a short time the group dissolved. One of the members of the group told me, with shame:

"If they knew that we are talking here in a group, the management of the factory would dismiss us, and then we would even lose our flats."

I saw it was time to leave the settlement.

I went back again in 1992. The people said that while the style of management remained the same there were some changes: more people had become unemployed and it was uncertain whether the company would stay in business. They were informed about nothing. They had only fear: what would happen to them? Where would they go; what would they do? First of all we clarified what was required:

(1)   to get information about the possible decisions of the company

(2)   to consider the consequences of the coming change of proprietorship: the problem of the flats and the communal building ownership

(3)   to address the problem of unemployment.

The new management, charged with the completion of privatisation and being afraid of the media, was under considerable pressure to meet with the local inhabitants. On this occasion the management informed the people that the process of selling the flats could not be stopped and if the tenant-inhabitants did not buy the flats they were obliged to sell them to anyone else. The communal rooms did not belong to the company any more and the local government was responsible for solving their financial problems. The different parts of the company were to be privatised separately and independently to anyone interested. This could not be achieved here since farming had virtually stopped. The local government had to offer something, because this problem was also their responsibility.

The next step was to deal with the issues and feelings arising from the sale of the flats. The question for the people was whether or not to buy. Finally, it was decided, through mediation, that the flats, which had been valued earlier as almost worthless, were to be sold for one-third of the price originally designated. The company refused very firmly to sell the land. So finding a solution to the problem of unemployment seemed hopeless.

During this period the dynamics of the group accelerated and the idea of creating a civil organisation, an association, no longer seemed impossible. The attempt to establish a relationship with the local government ended in failure: they not only refused the compromises offered by the company but they announced that they did not accept the settlement on behalf of the village. So they were not willing to have anything in common with the inhabitants of the settlement although they belonged administratively to the village. Meanwhile, with the help of one of the partners of the company, an association had been established. This association felt its power, and its members started to negotiate with the company's leaders with a feeling of strength.

Selling the communal buildings was the next step. The company wanted to get themselves out of that issue, so the local inhabitants and representatives of local government and of the company had a meeting. It was held in a building which was the only collective gathering place for the settlement's 100 inhabitants. While the negotiations continued about the ownership of that building all the furniture was sold or burnt by the employees of the company.

I invited the TV and the Press into this cold, shabby room, using the pressure of publicity to force the representatives of local government and the company to take responsibility for the situation. This produced results. The media, and the large number of questions asked by an organised group of my colleagues, forced the management to sell the most important communal buildings to the association for a token sum. The buildings could have been given free of charge to the local government, but its representatives rejected this possibility in a letter. That letter was produced and this broke the intransigence of the representatives; their arrogant reactions were only self-justification, and their single argument was that the local government did not have enough money. After this explosion the association declared that the legal status of the settlement should be made clear; that it was part of the area of the local government. This meant that residents had a right to get their financial share of the local government's budget.

After that climax, relations started to soften and the local government offered the amount necessary to buy the buildings. In the refurnished rooms there were cultural activities and a weaving studio and I started to facilitate a framework for collective activity. I was looking for non-profit organisations abroad to help in selling the products outside of the local market. The studio started enthusiastically with the leadership of an expert, but after some weeks only a few women went on with the weaving and they too lost their motivation.

3. Another project: 1993 The small village
Within the framework of a new project I was trying to research the social conditions in villages with gypsy inhabitants. Choosing the place required the co-operation of the local government and especially the mayor.

After receiving preliminary information from the mayor it became clear that the most serious problem in the village was unemployment which affected both gypsies and non-gypsies. After the first meeting (with the villagers) the next one was held only for the unemployed. In that meeting I said that I was not able to solve their problem alone; the participation of those affected was also necessary. They had to come up with ideas and possible solutions. After a short period of hesitation and distrust the group of ten, mainly women, who represented only one-third of the unemployed, started to express their ideas in a tentative way, such as growing of medicinal herbs, making and preserving food products, intensive gardening, or learning a new craft, including basket-making. I suggested that they should organise small groups under the leadership of the developers of the different ideas. One of the group leaders became the practical organiser of the plans, and I began getting information and conferring with the mayor, who was available by phone.

The mayor offered several ideas to improve the situation in the village but at the same time he expressed doubt whether the ideas would succeed. He suggested they should open a local discount grocery, resettle the local school, and use the empty buildings belonging to the church. All the projects died in the same way as did his offer of help for creating a food-product workshop. Even in the first phase he emphasised that he would not be able to deal with another business because it would compete with his own.

There were three people in the village who had larger farms: the mayor, who had animals; an elderly farmer who had revitalised his farm with the help of compensation; and a third belonging to one of the representatives who was experimenting with up-to-date vegetable production in his own garden. Her husband is a technical employee in the farmers' co-operative. At his request I was looking for an expert to offer a course on intensive farming for a small group. By the time it was due to start, the interest in it had died out. The initiator of the programme tried hard to persuade me that possibilities existed for all who really wanted to solve their problems instead of waiting for benefits. The style of this argument was reminiscent of earlier cant in which the people were blamed for the circumstances of their backward lives.

The lack of empathy and responsibility was less daunting than in the previous village, but the mayor's lack of real interest gradually demonstrated that the local inhabitants were to be left to their own resources. The lack of real co-operation from the mayor showed when I asked him, by phone, to pass on the first important piece of information, the address of a herb production expert. Some weeks later when I inquired whether the expert had been found at the address I had given, they did not know what I was talking about.

Some women kept up their interest in medicinal-herb production and they went to the representative of that company. Unfortunately they were not able to go further. The number of women involved was gradually diminishing but two of them remained very active and kept our co-operation strong. During one conversation one of them explained how she had attempted to challenge the village's passivity. She described a situation where the village's families were unwilling to go either to pleasant and friendly meetings or to the programmes organised for their children. Although she and the other woman seemed to be confident and to have adequate self-esteem, both were inclined to use their energy to work for a social allowance, which, at that time, was lacking. I was determined to create situations that forced them to help each other and in that way to share activities until we could develop some concrete collective purposes. The second woman mentioned took the leading role and she became the engine of the organising success.

As the winter was coming I was looking for a programme concerned with making some sort of handicraft. I invited a folk-industrial artist and I suggested that these two women should organise people interested from the circle of gypsy inhabitants. I also invited an American student who was studying in Hungary on a scholarship at that time, and he offered a conflict-resolution training programme for children. In the course of individual talks, a lot of dissatisfaction was focused on the mayor who kept his distance from the programmes, could not be found to answer any questions or requests, and who had no time to deal with the matters of the community. His distance and lack of interest led to the first display of intense and serious emotions when I invited a manufacturer who dealt with making toys. The mayor offered to get wood materials for the workshop and to organise unemployed men for that workshop. By the time we arrived there were only two women, who had been informed about our coming some minutes earlier. In that situation the manufacturer offered only the most simple routine work for the women. Only one of them took it up but after some months she gave up because of the low pay.

With the leadership of the American student, we organised an afternoon party for children in which some of my students were involved.

Then the second woman of the two, mentioned above, finished a business course and found that she could count on neither the group programmes nor the support of the mayor. She started with her husband to run a small discount shop in a separate part of their house. To achieve the establishment of her shop she needed financial support, but the mayor refused to help. Some families in the village offered to help them extend the building of their shop if the financial and legal background of it could be guaranteed. The small shop had only a few goods but it seemed to become a meeting place for the neighbourhood and to satisfy real needs with its lower prices. The rejection and indifference of the local officers encouraged independent action. There were possibilities which arose from having an association and I obtained information about applications that could be made for financial support for programmes that would provide work and employment. However, the bureaucratic difficulties of building the little shop could only partly be solved and, considering the initial high hopes not only for a shop but for a small confectionery as well, this was a bitter disappointment.

The most active woman keeps going on with the association: she writes applications to start programmes for employment but she has become exhausted in the struggle. Our co-operation has been reduced to her personal support. The medicinal-herb production brought disappointment as well: the very hard work has produced only a minimal salary.

The best part of this experience was a summer camp for children organised by the American student, who has now unfortunately left Hungary. The next programme we are planning aims to revitalise the life of the association; we want to have people recognised in the forthcoming local government elections for their own active roles and the experiences they have gained. We are going to prepare for these tasks and I have been asked to give support. At the next meeting a local government expert will inform the association members about the law.

Theory and practice
There is a split between the institutions of civil society and representative democracy. This situation has the consequence of dividing society into two parts; those who are directing the political processes and those who are outside of them. In this way the political split can become reflected in the social split. The conclusion to be drawn from these projects is that, in this period of transition, it is necessary to empower the local societies to organise themselves into civil organisations, although that is not without problems. But in order not to undermine the institutions of representative democracy we have to interpret these actions as a learning process. This process involves community work as an intervention into the life of communities.

Individual and group empowerment involves a process which I call - in a metaphorical sense - a "talk". Talk, for those who are intervening, is a source of information. For those who are involved, it is a way of discovering the power of individual and group presence through conflicts. In this process some people can legitimate themselves through separation from others while some find the opportunity to join others and in this way to discover their own capacities. Talk is the tool for finding the definition of the situation and the shape of possible solutions (Godamer 1984). I found that to ask questions can be a tool for empowerment for those who have no experience of being asked their views by someone with a genuine interest.

I would suggest that there are two feelings underlying the rejection of political parties by the people: the parties represent the divisions in society. For those communities which are disintegrated the activities of the parties would lead to serious conflicts. There is a deep fear of these conflicts.

The other root of rejection lies in the differences between the functional situation of parties and of citizens. The parties want to be attractive to citizens, therefore they do not ask questions but make declarations about themselves. They speak a different language. This language barrier prevents communication and therefore prevents access to the resources without which communities cannot act.. The empowerment of civil society can lead in this context to powerful communication between citizens and political representatives.

Bibliography
Berger, P. L. and Luckmann, T. (1979) *The Social Construction of Reality*. London: Penguin.

Berlin, I. (1969) *Four essays about liberty*. London: Oxford University Press.

de Tocqueville, A. (1988) *Democracy in America*. New York: Harper & Row.

Dewey, J. (1992) *The Democracy and America*. Budapest: Condolat.

Godamer, H. G. (1984) *Truth and Method*.

Pateman, C. (1970) *Participation and Democratic Theory*. Cambridge: Cambridge University Press.

Szücs, J. (1983) *Schedule of the three historical regions of Europe*. Budapest: Magvetó.

Notes
1.   I am using Isaiah Berlin's concept of negative freedom. He defined it as freedom from intervention by any power, including the State.

2. Pateman, C. in his work Participation and Democratic Theory explains the participatory theories of Rousseau, J.S. Mill and G.D.H. Cole. He derives the functions of participation from the Social Contract.

3. Szücs, J., a Hungarian historian, analysed these tendencies and the consequences of this development: "Does it belong to this tendency the special disharmonical, depressive opposite of rebellious self-suggestion, . . . the resigned acquiescence in the given situation because the decisions in all important issues should be made 'upstairs'?"

4. With the concept of "everyday life" I am referring to the writing of Berger, P.L. and Luckmann, T. on the sociology of knowledge and the social construction of reality.

5. Dewey, J., analysing the American traditions, focused on the empowerment of local communities. He quotes from Thomas Jefferson who emphasised the importance of local community: "Democracy has to begin at home; the home is the neighbourhood."

6. de Tocqueville, A.: In explaining the democracy in America he defines the local community as the basic institution of the whole political system.

7. Godamer, H.G., in his work about Hermeneutik, analyses the rules of dialogue. Its most important component is the question.

Empowerment Under Capitalism:
The Case of the United States

Ram A. Cnaan

Summary

This chapter assumes that certain kinds of both capitalism and voluntary action are basic tenets of democracy. The freedom to own property as well as the freedom to choose where, when, and to what extent to assist any cause are manifestations of individual rights and empowerment. The chapter acknowledges that capitalism has many negative side-effects which include, among others, power of employers over employees, threat to individual expression in the work-place, ongoing competition at the expense of individuals and communities, oppression of and discrimination against minority groups, and inherent inequality. The United States is presumed to be the best example of capitalist society, and it suffers from the above maladies. However, through the extraordinary amount of volunteer involvement and a rich tradition of voluntary organisations, the quality of community life is preserved in some parts of the United States. The chapter concludes with policy recommendations for societies that are undertaking the capitalist route, cautioning them to be sure to invest in civil society by enhancing their voluntary sectors.

Although it is beyond the scope of this chapter to present and analyse Capitalism as a social and political system, some reflections on the tenets of Capitalism are required in order to examine empowerment possibilities in the United States. The Capitalist system is predicated under a certain set of assumptions, most of which are only partially exercised in any so-called "Capitalist State". The central tenet of Capitalism (or as Europeans call it, "Liberalism") is that in order to achieve the maximum benefits of the collective, individuals should compete to maximise individual profit. It is assumed that if producers compete with each other, then better and cheaper products will be produced, and the needs of individuals and families will optimally be met. Thus, implied in this state of constant competition is the principle of economic individualism.

Under this principle, each adult or family unit is expected to produce an income sufficient to meet its needs without being dependent on others. Furthermore, inequality in income is accepted and even valued as it is interpreted as an indicator of one's success and contribution. Thus, disparity in income represents a continuum of success and failure in life's key goal. Kluegel and Smith (1986), based on a national survey, concluded that: "American culture contains a stable, widely held set of beliefs involving the availability of opportunity, individualistic explanations of achievement, and acceptance of unequal distribution of rewards" (p.11). Thus, following the principle of economic individualism is the belief that one is not responsible for the welfare of another unless the other person is a family member or is related in some other way; another possibility is that the person feels benevolent and is willing to help the other financially. Finally, in order to guarantee a smooth economic and social system, the government should be as small as possible, should keep taxes as low as possible, and should not regulate the market, i.e., the Lockean principle of suspected government which represents inefficiency and suppression.

As noted above, no one society fully exercises Capitalism, but the society that comes closest is the United States of America. Capitalism is part of the American dream. Many studies have documented that even people who are poor and deprived in the U.S.A. embrace the premise of inequality and economic individualism. One well-studied result of the Capitalist system is a very limited and punitive welfare system. In America, a large segment of the poor are regarded as unworthy, and consequently welfare is very limited; homelessness is an accepted way of life affecting some three million residents a year (Culhane *et al.*, 1994), and suggestions to cut welfare to mothers who become pregnant while on welfare are the norm rather than the exception. It is of no surprise that as a result of the 1994 elections both Democrats andRepublicans are ready to cut welfare allocations which already are among the lowest of any of the modern industrial democracies.

The question is, how is it for the majority of people to live under Capitalism? What are the domains of life in which people can practise individuality and feel empowered? One such possibility may be the work-place. As the value of opportunity and mobility is so high in the American value system, one would expect work to be the arena where many Americans exercise empowerment. However, the reality is somewhat different. Most adults in the U.S.A. are employed by private organisations to perform tasks. In the Capitalist system, these people are dependent on their monthly (for some weekly or bi-weekly) pay-check in order to guarantee an ongoing livelihood. This dependency is typical of most modern societies. Without a continuous income, loan payments will not be made property may be seized, and one's personal financial record will be tainted. Ask any group of people, with the exception of the most affluent members of society, how long they can survive without a paycheck; the answer will usually range from one to six months, with an average of two months. While most respondents acknowledge that they have credit lines and the ability to postpone payments, they also recognise that they will acquire multiple debts in this situation. It is obvious that some who lose work may be eligible for unemployment benefits which will prolong the above estimations, but unemployment benefits in the U.S.A. are lower than one's salary and are short term.

Most people under the Capitalist system are, willingly though not necessarily consciously, buried under a large array of debts or ongoing payments. Capitalist societies encourage their members to consume beyond their means and, thus, to take out long-term loans. Those in Capitalist societies who follow the average lifestyle take long-term mortgages (or pay monthly rents), buy a car and pay for it in anywhere from three to five years (or lease one and pay a monthly fee), pay membership to certain associations and groups, subscribe to journals, magazines, and/or newspapers, pay monthly premiums for health insurance, take very-long-term loans to finance higher education, and purchase food and clothing. This description will not sound strange or out of the ordinary to anyone who has lived in any modern society, so why is it worth mentioning?

People in the U.S.A. who move through the life cycle, acquire, very early in life, financial responsibilities which grow larger as time goes on. One who puts money into a down-payment for a house and agrees to pay a certain mortgage must meet that mortgage on a monthly basis. Similarly, responsible parents in America take it upon themselves to guarantee the cost of a college education for their children, one which is currently estimated at $100,000 for the undergraduate degree. The most common source of income for such ongoing payments is income from work. This creates an enormous dependency for most citizens on their employers. This is especially so when people are not guaranteed work and have very little employment-related protection or job security. In a Capitalist society, one can lose his or her work with little notice. Many companies are now in the process of downsizing, that is, laying off thousands of employees regardless of their seniority, contribution, or needs. While many companies encourage early retirement, equally others find it easier to cut units and/or production sites. The value underlining this phenomenon is that the employer does not owe anything to the employee, and the latter is paid and employed only as long as it is beneficial to the employer.

It is quite acceptable in the United States for people to receive a pink slip on Friday which means "we do not need you any more, do not come back to work on Monday". The end result is that people are very careful not to assert themselves against their superiors and feel powerless and alienated. The high dependency on income from work, both as a social value and as a necessity to retain a certain standard of living, makes it devastating to lose a job. One's sense of pride and fulfilment is threatened when a job is lost. American workers know that they have to comply with job requirements and that their job security is very limited. Thus, on the average, a worker in the U.S.A. feels quite powerless on the job.

One interesting exception to this description of the powerless working environment is the issue of salary bargaining. While lower class people are subjected to either a minimum wage (which is very minimal) or welfare (even below minimum wage), middle and upper class Americans are, usually, bargaining for their salary on their own. Most Americans do not participate in collective bargaining, and thus their income is determined by individual negotiation with their employer or supervisor. This mechanism enables many Americans to assert themselves and be measured according to their value and ability to bargain on their own behalf. Consequently, one's salary in American society (with the exception of Civil Servants) is a secret kept between the employee and employer. Two workers in the same room who are doing the same work would not be surprised to learn that their salaries are markedly distinct. While it is very individualistic in nature and provides many Americans with power (or at least the feeling of power), in reality, for many groups, it is an experience of powerlessness. It has been shown in many studies that women and minorities in particular are less effective in representing themselves, regardless of the quality and value of their work, and are paid less due to a deficiency in bargaining skills.

There are people who take risks, assert themselves, and try to rise to the top. Ultimately, they either lose their job or succeed. If they succeed, then they reach a stage in which they can minimise the power of others; that is, they employ others and keep the power of their employees at a minimum. This is not to say that all American workers are powerless, abused and depressed. There are many who are doing quite well, especially professionals. Most importantly, however, is the fact that the American value system justifies and perpetuates such relationships between workers and employers. It is accepted that for the society to function and for the American dream to continue, employers should exercise full power to limit their employees' tenure to as long as is needed, and it is the responsibility of individual workers to be economically independent at all times, regardless of employment status.

Thus, work is not the arena in which most residents of the United States manifest empowerment. Empowerment, for the sake of this chapter, is the individual ability and actualisation of doing what one sees as his or her wish without being severely punished. Empowerment is one's ability to decide and act in accordance with his or her interests and preferences without being pressured or coerced by others to act differently. From all of the above, it is clear that Americans do not exercise empowerment at work. Yet, an inherent value of the American Capitalist society is individual freedom, minimum state (and for that matter any other external) interference with one's life, and the dream to quit one's job and wander. Clearly, the working conditions of America and the American value system are incompatible. Or, put it differently, empowerment, for most Americans, is not exercised in the world of work, and if it exists it does so elsewhere.

I was not born in the U.S.A. and thus look at it from a focal point of life in another culture. When I came to the United States as an adult and as a professional, I was amazed at how the local society was managed. The local and national governments are treated jointly and have very little to do with civic life. Thousands of activities that together constitute civic life are performed by endless volunteers and voluntary organisations, a phenomenon that may not be uniquely American, but in no other country has it reached such a proportion.

As a consequence of the Capitalist interest (the Lockean principle) of keeping government small and out of people's business, taxes in the United States are relatively low and, consequently, public sector services are very limited. For example, when I moved into my new house, my 10-year-old son wanted to play soccer. In many other countries he would have either had go out to play informally in the neighborhood field (if such a field existed) or would join a group coached by an employee of the city recreation department. In our neighborhood, the only venue for playing soccer was a nonprofit organisation. This nonprofit organisation has a board of trustees composed of some 20 volunteers who are interested in soccer and who are willing to contribute both time and money to enhance the sport of soccer in America. These trustees hired one manager to organise a league. The league operates from September to November. Parents who want their children to play pre-register in the summer and pay a participation fee which supports the manager's salary as well as paying for uniforms for all players and other needed team equipment. Every year, this nonprofit organisation has over 100 teams of about 18 players. Each team needs a coach and an assistant coach. These 200 individuals are parents who volunteer to coach the team once a week and to manage it on Saturday in a game. Thus, in order to supply children with an opportunity to play soccer and to enhance the game's popularity, a special nonprofit organisation was created by people who like playing and teaching soccer; a manager who likes soccer was hired, and 200 parents volunteered four hours a week to assist. It should be emphasised that no parent was forced to become a coach, and no parent was paid for coaching. However, a normative expectation was established: in order for this project to take-off, 200 parents need to volunteer to coach and the same number must continue to volunteer each year if the program is to continue. Furthermore, if one is interested and lacks the necessary knowledge, the non-profit organisation provides proper training for beginner coaches.

This example can be further expanded as it conveys two major facets of the American Capitalist system - facets where one can find major avenues for empowerment. Firstly, the massive reliance on nonprofit (voluntary) organisations rather than relying on governmental services, as a means for people to act on their behalf and follow their interests. Secondly, the high status and expectation of people to volunteer are a means of expressed empowerment.

In the United States when an individual is concerned about any issue, the most likely avenue for action is to form a group of interested citizens. These organisations range from environmental to educational, from religious to social, from literary to musical, and they cover virtually every aspect of social life in the United States. Prestby and Wandersman (1985) found that, in many areas as small as a block and as large as a neighborhood, people form informal, and at times formal, associations to represent the interests of residents *vis-à-vis* city departments, transportation authorities, plans to move hazardous materials into the neighborhood, crime, or utility companies (gas and electricity). In almost every American school there is a parent-teacher association which, despite its name, is basically an organisation of parents who agree to represent other parents *vis-à-vis* the school and who are expected to influence the curriculum as well as to be involved in the day-to-day running of the school. Parents who wish to get even more involved can opt for an alternative school in which parents, in cooperation with teachers, set the full curriculum and may come and teach many of the classes on a regular basis. In such a school, parents meet extensively with teachers and guide them as to content of specific classes, educational material to be used, means of assessing if children understand the covered material, and disciplinary actions.

People in the U.S.A. do not trust their government nor do they expect government to assist in performing tasks which serve the goals of small groups. Government is expected to intervene in matters that affect all citizens, otherwise it will be a form of discrimination. Consequently, people with particular tastes cannot expect public authorities to serve their needs, but they can attempt to influence these authorities or to produce the desired goods themselves. Furthermore, the most common avenue for individuals to influence their environment and to become more powerful is through the voluntary joining and forming of nonprofit (voluntary) associations. The decision to form a group, which eventually may become a voluntary association, is legally guaranteed in the American constitution and is an accepted norm. Furthermore, the American tax system has a special status for voluntary organisations which is very simple and easy to follow. Nonprofit organisations of all sorts mail in an application form to be designated as such, a request which is almost never denied, and from there on pay lower taxes. Thus, not only does the normative system enhance empowerment through community organising, but the tax system also supports it. The Internal Revenue Service (1995) reported that in 1993 there were 1,118,118 tax exempt organisations in the United States. Approximately one-half of them are voluntary organisations while the rest are large universities, hospitals, and agricultural groups; yet, even half of that figure means a very large number of nonprofit organisations, each with its own board of trustees, each carrying out a unique mission independently of the government or the private sector.

Active people who are concerned with any issue can assert themselves and become more powerful by forming groups. These groups are purely voluntary in the sense that anyone interested in the subject can join; there is no coercion to do so, and people can leave the group at any point in time. In fact, people who are most concerned with a certain issue attempt to recruit additional members. Mondros and Wilson (1993) noted that "involving, engaging, and sustaining a large and strongly identified group of participants is important to achieving organisational goals" (pp.69-70).

Often, the interested members contribute both time and/or money to enhance their common cause. As taxes are relatively low in the U.S.A., many people donate money to numerous causes, a fact which, again, is supported by the tax system as each donation (with the exception of political ones) is also tax exempted. Furthermore, a strong correlation was found between being active with any group and financially contributing to this group (Hodgkinson and Weitzman, 1992). Financial support for various causes and groups is not limited to affluent members of the American society. In fact, it is a way for all people to assert themselves and support issues in which they believe, such as helping old people in the neighborhood, advancing certain ethnic group status, protecting rights of certain groups, supporting the arts, and many other issues which are of importance to the people. There is no pressure to donate money, nor is there a legal requirement to do so.

In fact, people donate unequally, and everyone who ever donated money is expected to be solicited by numerous organisations and causes. Thus, one chooses among many potential causes and organisations which one finds personally appealing and worthy and donates accordingly. Thus, in a Capitalistic country such as the United States, low taxes enable people to be empowered to donate money to a cause of their choice and, in the process, strengthen an organisation that may serve and protect their interests.

It should be noted that the opportunity to form such voluntary organisations is not restricted to a certain ideological stream. In the United States both "Pro-life" and "Pro-choice" started as small voluntary groups and are still operated as nonprofit organisations. Those interested in hunting deer and those who want to prevent killing deer are organised as voluntary organisations.

It is up to any individual to find an area of interest, to assess what group may represent his or her interests, and to join and become active in the group. This mode of action enables Americans to feel empowered and in control of their environment, even though, for many, work is a repressing environment. Empowerment is manifested, to a large degree, outside of work and in joining or forming such voluntary associations. Numerous studies (cf. Smith, 1994) show that people of higher socio-economic status take advantage of the opportunity to join voluntary associations more than those in the lower social strata. Furthermore, Smith suggested that participation is generally greater for individuals who are characterised by a more dominant set of positions and roles, both ascribed and achieved, such as being a male, highly educated, married, middle or upper class, middle-aged, physically healthy, non-impaired, long-time resident, employed full-time, and high in occupational status. However, this is not to say that joining voluntary associations is solely reserved for middle and upper class members of society. In the 1960s, Piven and Cloward (1977) demonstrated how thousands of poor people joined together to put pressure on government to make various welfare programs more accessible, and generous. For as long as these voluntary organisations were active, welfare payments were indeed more accessible and generous; however, once these groups felt that they had achieved their goals and gradually dissolved, welfare payments once more became less access ible and their purchasing power decreased. Similarly, regardless of socio-economic background, millions of Americans are members of religious congregations. In the United States, where State and Church are legally and practically separated, religious congregations serve a broader function than in many other countries. Members of congregations form many committees and task forces to carry out what is often called social ministry. That is, members of religious congregations set out to influence their communities by performing a variety of activities that add to the quality of life in the community. Congregations play a critical role in community life. Day care services, Alcoholics Anonymous meetings, services for the homeless, religious teaching, choirs, and many other important activities are performed by individuals who organise under the auspices of religious congregations which enable people to control and influence their immediate environment rather than be victims.

Many congregations provide human services to their members or the larger community and employ volunteers. Wineburg (1990-1), in a study of 128 congregations in Greensboro, North Carolina, found that, on average, each congregation provided five different services. Eighty-four percent offered at least one in-house service, and 87% provided volunteer or other in-kind support for one or more human service activities in the community. Among the services were soup kitchens, shelters, day care, health services, counselling, transportation, and tutoring. Filinson (1988) documented how a mental health centre trained and used church volunteers from an interfaith coalition to provide services to people with Alzheimer's disease. Negstead and Arnholt (1986) noted the cooperation between local church-based day care centers for the elderly and members of the local community services system. Finally, Shelp, DuBose, and Sunderland (1990) reported that "Teams of volunteers from individual congregations are recruited and trained to provide social support, physical care, emotional support, and spiritual care to dependent, home-based patients [of AIDS] and their loved ones" (p.970). They also reported that over a two-year period, 650 volunteers in Houston provided help, valued at $584,000 to 486 patients. The project's success led to its replication in many cities. These many activities are only a few examples of how residents voluntarily join together in exerting influence over their own lives and the lives of those in the surrounding community.

Another important avenue for Americans to feel and practice empowerment is through volunteering. Volunteerism, defined as a social phenomenon of unpaid care and citizen participation in society, is highly regarded in all parts of the world. Again, volunteering is not uniquely American, but what is unique about it in the United States is its scope. In a given year, more than half of the American adult population volunteer to assist others. On the average, each of these volunteers is providing 4.2 hours of service a week. One-sixth of the adult American population (13.6%) can be described as being committed to volunteering by providing, on the average, more than five hours of volunteer work a week.

In total, it is estimated that 20.5 billion hours in both formal and informal volunteering were given in 1991. These 20.5 billion hours are equivalent to about 10 million paid full-time positions, with an estimated worth of $176 billion in 1991. This is clearly an impressive manifestation of the commitment to volunteerism and its importance in American society (Hodgkinson and Weitzman, 1992).

People in the United States are volunteering for multiple roles. The range of volunteering goes from helping a sick elderly neighbour to being the chairperson of a nonprofit organisation's board of trustees (Cnaan and Amrofell, 1995). People volunteer by the thousands for any possible cause ranging from environmental protection to enhancing ethnic dances. Multiple activities and causes that in many less Capitalistic countries would have been performed by government are left for individual volunteers to carry out if they seem relevant and worthy.

Because so many people volunteer in the United States, a decision to volunteer may seem an easy one and less of an individual statement. In a society where in any given year, about half of the adult population report that they engage in a volunteer activity, to volunteer is more to comply with a social norm than to act individually. In a country in which presidents from both the left (Kennedy and Clinton) and the right (Reagan and Bush) call for people to volunteer, and schools and colleges require students to volunteer, being a volunteer is an expected behavior that requires no explanation. Thus, one may see in volunteerism yet another social obligation put upon people which supports the Capitalist structure.

However, volunteerism has an important role in providing people with empowerment opportunities. Volunteerism, in the American context, is viewed as both a means and an expression of a democratic society and freedom of choice. Democratic societies value freedom of choice, the opportunity to make one's own decisions, quest for space and for uniqueness, belief in self-actualisation, and drive for success. Volunteerism, in that respect, provides people with opportunities for individual choice, and the success that volunteering offers increases one's self-actualisation. Volunteering is only possible if it is a personal decision and investment, if it is unrewarded financially, and if those who volunteer value freedom of choice. The decision to become a volunteer is an individual one and so is the decision to choose the agency or cause for which to volunteer. It is in this way that volunteers all over the world practice their freedom of choice on a daily basis by assisting others though they are neither required to do so nor penalised if they do not. As long as people are choosing freely, democracy is served. On the other hand, collective compulsory volunteering often involves coercion and, as such, is not considered truly voluntary action and diminishes one's sense of empowerment.

Wuthnow (1991) noted that freedom to do what one wants is the most prized of all of the American possessions. It is not only the freedom to choose a government, but at the individual level, "it constitutes a basic right to individual autonomy. It means not having anyone tell us what to do, not having to listen if they do, not having to conform. It means having the capacity to make our own decisions, rather than simply living up to the expectations of the community or fulfilling obligations to someone else" (p.12). Wuthnow went on to stress the importance of self-interest and the struggle for individual success as key tenets of the American value system. He further noted that volunteerism can easily be seen as antithetical to this value system. Thus, a conflict may exist between individualism and compassion. For Wuthnow, an individualistic society, such as the American society, is not expected to be deeply concerned about the welfare of others. Wuthnow sought to solve this tension by focusing on the rewards, from opportunities for individual choice to the volunteer control over the length and magnitude of commitment, and the success that volunteering offers as a means of expressing one's control and individuality. Similarly, one may decide that she or he no longer wishes to volunteer. This is not individual heroism *à la* the Lone Ranger, but rather an individual choice in everyday life. This is what Stevenson and Parsloe (1993) noted when they wrote "we believe that the goal of empowerment, realised through having the opportunity to make decisions is not only about big decisions, it is also about small ones" (p.8).

Wuthnow further asserted that people gain a sense of fulfilment from volunteering but that it is not directly related to those helped. What he failed to see is that those helped serve as a catalyst for the volunteer: people need to get in touch with those who need help if they are to realise the potential for fulfilment in volunteering. In this respect both parties benefit, and caring relationships in the community are set into motion. "When someone shows compassion to a stranger, it does set in motion a series of relationships that spreads throughout the entire society" (p. 300). Thus, compassion and care in the Capitalist U.S.A. may be selfishly motivated, but they set the tone and the basis for a complex web of individual commitments and a rich civic life that is based on people's freedom to get involved and to actively support whatever is dear to their hearts.

As a final contribution to this chapter, I would like to caution all those that embrace American style Capitalism for its economic aspect alone. The American society is not more altruistic and compassionate than any other society. In fact, Americans believe that inequality is justified, and the work ethic is primary in the American way of life. Public support for welfare, with the exception of insurance type programs, is very low. Yet, millions of people are engaged in being members of voluntary organisations, donating money to various groups, and volunteering to enhance numerous causes. Thus, the American Capitalistic system is a complex and multilayered one. Beneath the ruthless economic and labor systems there are many societal systems that together constitute a unique system of care, involvement, and multiple opportunities to feel and practice empowerment. Copying the American Capitalist system into a different country should not end with free market, open competition, dis-empowering workers, and worshipping inequality; it should also include the adoption of individual and corporate responsibility to guarantee a civic society in which individuals can feel empowered to organise and support whatever causes they wish.

References

Cnaan, R. A.and Amrofell, L. (1995). Mapping volunteer activity. *Nonprofit and Voluntary Sector Quarterly*, 23(4), forthcoming.

Culhane, D. P; Dejowski, E. F; Ibanez, J; Needham, E. and Macchia, I. (1994). Public shelter admission rates in Philadelphia and New York City: The implications of turnover for sheltered population counts. *Housing policy debates*, 5, 107-140.

Filinson, R. (1988). A model for church-based services for frail and elderly persons and their families. *The Gerontologist*, 28, 483-486.

Hodgkinson, V. A. and Weitzman, M. S. (1992). *Giving and volunteering in the United States*. Washington, D. C. Independent Sector.

Internal Revenue Service (1995). *The Commissioner's annual report for 1993.* Washington, D.C. Superintendent of Documents, U.S. Government Printing Office.

Kluegel, J. R. and Smith, E. R. (1986). *Beliefs about inequality: Americans view of what is and what ought to be*. New York: Aldine de Gruyter.

Mondros, J.B. and Wilson, S.M. (1993). Building high access community organizations: Structures as strategy. In T. Mizrahi and J. Morrison (Eds.), *Community organization and social administration: Advances, trends, and emerging principles* (pp.69-85). New York: Haworth.

Negstead, J. and Arnholt, R. (1986). Day centers for older adults: Parish and agency partnership. *Journal of Religion and Aging*, 4, 25-33.

Piven, F. F. and Cloward, R. A. (1977). *Poor people's movements: Why they succeed, why they fail*. New York: Vintage.

Prestby, J. and Wandersman, A. (1985). An empirical exploration of a framework of organizational viability: Maintaining block associations. *Journal of Applied Behavioral Science*, 21, 287-305.

Shelp, E. E., DuBose, E. R., & Sunderland, R. H. (1990). The infrastructure of religious communities: A neglected resource for care of people with AIDS. *American Journal of Public Health, 80,* 970-972.

Smith, D. H. (1994). Determinants of voluntary association participation and volunteering: A literature review. *Nonprofit and Voluntary Sector Quarterly, 23,* 243-263.

Stevenson, O., & Parsloe, P. (1993). *Community care and empowerment.* York, UK: Joseph Rowntree Foundation.

Wineburg, R. J. (1990-1). A community study on the ways religious congregations support individuals and human service network. *The Journal of Applied Social Sciences,* 15 (1), 51-74.

Wuthnow, R. (1991). Acts of compassion: *Caring for others and helping ourselves.* Princeton, N. J. Princeton University Press.

Empowerment Practice in Social Work:
The Case of Hong Kong

Kwong Wai Man

Summary

Empowerment is a new concept introduced to the social work profession in Hong Kong in the last couple of years. This concept has been embraced by social workers in the West for its moral appeal and yet has not been critically examined for conceptual clarity and its meaning for practice. Empowerment is being used loosely and yet exists more in professional discourse than in actual practice. The same seems to be happening in Hong Kong. In this light, the author cautions the uncritical adoption of western social work concepts by local social workers. The paper begins with a critical analysis of the concept of empowerment and the issue of professional power in empowerment practice. The main part of the paper examines empowerment practice in community work in Hong Kong, followed by a discussion of the findings drawn from an exploratory study of the conception of good practice held by family service workers. Good practice in family service includes empowerment practice as one of its elements.

The concept of empowerment is on the horizon, if not at the centre stage, in the social work discourse in Hong Kong. The concept has found its way into the training institutions that reproduce social work practice through the education of future social workers. Back in the early 70s when I received my social work education, this concept had never been heard of. Two decades later, now that I have become a social work teacher, I picked up this concept from my students three years ago in a seminar module on social work theories and practice. The aim of this module was to provide an intellectual space for the students to examine practice concepts and professional issues of their own choice. Several of my students chose "empowerment" as their seminar topic. What intrigued me was that this concept had not yet been picked up by social workers in the field at that time. I realised that once again, social work teachers had transplanted a new concept to the local social work profession. At the time this paper was written, a professional seminar was being held for both the users and practitioners involved in the rehabilitation service. The theme of the keynote speech was empowerment, and the composition of the reaction panel had something to tell us about this concept. It comprised an academic social worker, the Director of Social Welfare of the government, an administrator of a non-government organisation providing a rehabilitation service, a person with learning difficulties, and a representative of a parents association of a special school for children with learning difficulties, a condition still known in Hong Kong as mental retardation.

A review of western social work literature reveals how pervasive this concept of empowerment is in dominating social work practice in a variety of settings. Indeed, empowerment has become the mission and the goal of social work practice. It is interesting to note how ideas come and go in social work discourse. However, it is beyond the scope of this paper to examine why and how the concept of empowerment has received such acclaim in western social work. Rather, the purpose of this paper is to examine the concept of empowerment in the social work practice in Hong Kong.

Social Work in Hong Kong: A Western Transplant
In my days as a social work student, the social work profession in Hong Kong indulged in debate about the mission of social work and strategies to achieve that mission. The debate was framed in dichotomous terms: whether the mission of social work was social control or social change, whether social work was remedial or reformist in focus, and whether the focus of change was the individual or the environment. What fuelled the debate and determined its character was the social work discourse in the west at that time.

Midgley (1981), in an analysis of the development of social work into an international profession, points out that this was realised through the spread of colonial rule over the Third World in the first half of this century. Britain, as a major colonial power in those days, was responsible for transplanting western institutions, such as education, health, and social welfare, to her colonies in Asia and Africa. Hong Kong, being a British colony for the last 198 years, is a notable case. However, organised social welfare came into being only in the mid-50s and a rapid expansion took place in the early 70s when Hong Kong entered into a sustained period of economic growth.

It is not the concern here to examine the history of organised social welfare in Hong Kong. Suffice to say that it was amidst the growth of organised social welfare that the local social work profession emerged. Social workers started off as an occupational group in the post-war years when charitable organisations began to employ paid workers to provide relief and care to the poor, the sick, and the young who came as refugees from across the border after the defeat of the Nationalists by the Communists in China in 1949. This occupational group of relief and welfare workers acquired its professional status in the mid 60s when formal pre-service social work training was offered for the first time at the Chinese University of Hong Kong and, a few years later, at the University of Hong Kong. The professional association was established and so was the professional journal. Hence forth, Hong Kong had its institution dedicated to the reproduction of social work practice - though in the image of western social work.

According to Midgley (1981), it was through social work education that western social work was reproduced in the Third World countries after their independence in the post-war years. He cited two surveys on social work education in the developing world, which indicated that the social work curriculum in these countries was largely modelled after the curriculum of the schools of social work in the US and the UK. Hong Kong, in particular, was noted for the bias in her social work curriculum toward urban social work in the U.S. with strong emphasis on remedial and restorative work. It could not be otherwise since local social work educators in those early days were mostly expatriates or local people trained in the U.S. or the U.K. Given such historical antecedents, social work in Hong Kong was a transplant of western social work from the beginning. What is really intriguing is the fact that the reproduction of western social work has been perpetuated ever since, albeit the local social work education scene is now crowded with local social work teachers who had their initial, and occasionally their postgraduate, training in Hong Kong, and who practised for quite some years before they turned to teaching. Somehow, an indigenous conceptualisation of social work practice remains a distant vision.

Why is it that, throughout the last three decades since social work education was provided locally, social work educators have been reproducing western social work all the time? There are a number of reasons. First, it has something to do with the separation of theory from practice. The business of social work education is to equip students with the theories they use in practice. Thus, teaching in social work is foremost to teach theories, and the theories in stock are the theories produced in the West, in social science disciplines as well as in social work. Second, the seat of knowledge production has, for a long time, been located in the higher education institutions in the West. The circulation of knowledge among academics has been growing fast as a result of the proliferation of printed words through academic journals, books, and in recent years computer disks as well. Thus, social work teachers in Hong Kong actually belong to a large knowledge community of academic social workers in the West. Third, social work has achieved the status of an international profession, sharing a common culture and a practice grounded on a common body of knowledge and skills.

These are the reasons why social work teachers in Hong Kong have been so faithfully teaching western social work all these years.

However, social work teachers should be somewhat more critical than they have been thus far in transplanting the western model of social work to Hong Kong. The new (now not so new) awareness of ethnocentrism among social workers in the West should have cautioned against any uncritical adoption of new concepts and new practices into the local social work curriculum. Nevertheless, this is easier to say than to do. Being critical has to begin with an appreciation of the context that gives life to a new concept or a new practice. Unfortunately, critical discourse of this kind has been handicapped by the absence of such a premise, other than a concern with cultural difference. Culture, being an all encompassing and yet diffused concept, serves at best as an orienting concept rather than as a basis for critical analysis. Furthermore, new concepts and new practices are often introduced into the local social work discourse and are adopted almost intuitively, either for their moral appeal or for their promise to improve practice. Rarely was there any analysis of the particular context - be it historical, cultural, intellectual, or professional - that gave rise to a new concept or a new practice, or afforded the ground for it to take hold. Failing to appreciate such "contextual embeddedness" has given social workers in Hong Kong a false impression that they can adopt whatever concepts or practices they find appealing, without first evaluating whether they are appropriate to the local context. This is precisely the way in which empowerment, as a new concept, is being adopted by the social work profession in Hong Kong.

Empowerment: A New Concept? A Muddy Concept?
Empowerment is a new concept with the promise of leading to a new form of social work practice. First raised by Barbara Solomon (1976) in social work with oppressed communities in the US. in the 70s, this concept has acquired prominence in social work discourse in the West in the 80s. It has been imported into the local social work community in recent years. Its moral appeal is so obvious that it has received a warm reception from social workers in the West. In a culture that prizes the individual as a free agent, having control over one's life is an inalienable right, albeit this is something out of reach to many people. Increasingly public institutions claim more and more of the functions previously performed by mediating structures such as the family, the Church, the neighbourhood, and voluntary associations standing between the individual in his private life and the large institutions of public life (Berger & Neuhaus, 1977, p.2). It is the decline of society's mediating structures that results in people's sense of powerlessness (Kieffer, 1984). It is therefore no surprise that the concept of empowerment has

surged to a position of prominence in the professional discourse of social workers in the west. In these days, social work literature is flooded with the word empowerment. The term "empowering practice" is coined to connote an enlightened mode of practice by social workers in a variety of practice settings.

However, the popularity of this concept does not match its conceptual clarity. Scholars writing on the concept of empowerment have repeatedly cautioned the loose manner with which this concept is being used in social work discourse and in practice. Simon (1990) points out that "empowerment" has become a noble yet muddy term in social work theory and practice and there is urgent need to reduce conceptual confusion. The concept of empowerment has been widely embraced as the mission of social work practice in the last two decades. Nevertheless, Hartman (1993) notes that empowerment exists more in the professional discourse than in actual practice (p.365). Rees (1991) laments that "the word 'empowerment' has been and is being used as a term of convenience, to justify the maintenance of disempowering policies and practices rather than to achieve their elimination [and] a relatively new concept is being substituted for old ones without the political nature of empowerment being developed, with little indication of the way power is being defined or exercised . . ." (pp. 3 and 4). Despite these cautionary notes, the popularity of this concept has grown with time in social work literature and this by itself is a phenomenon of interest, though it is beyond the scope of this paper to analyse it.

What matters to the present discussion is that history seems to repeat itself as the concept of empowerment is gaining prominence in the social work discourse in Hong Kong. In view of the confusion in the way the concept of empowerment is being interpreted and translated into practice, there is an urgent need for the profession to undertake a critical analysis of empowering practice in the local context. The analysis that follows will try to seek clarity in the concept and practice of empowerment, advance a particular view of empowerment practice in Hong Kong, and examine the constraints on social workers aspiring to practice empowerment. It is hoped that this paper will stimulate dialogue among members of the social work community in Hong Kong and elsewhere.

Social Work and Empowerment: A Critical Analysis
The present analysis begins with the question: What is the meaning of empowerment? A common thread in various interpretations of this concept points to people acquiring a sense of control as well as actually taking control of their affairs. People who do not have that sense of control are beset by a feeling of powerlessness, and fall prey to the dictate of circumstances and the environment that

constrains them. The underlying view is that there are groups of people who are not able to take control of their lives or do not have such a sense of control because they have no power or because they perceive themselves as powerless. It is this connection between control and power (or lack of control and powerlessness) that suggests the political nature of empowerment. Rappaport (1987) defines empowerment as a process, a mechanism by which people, organisations, and communities gain mastery over their affairs (p.122). Furthermore, the process of acquiring power, holding power, and using it to control one's affairs, is a political one. In other words, empowerment practice in social work is political by nature. The outcome of empowerment practice may be expressed in tangible, material gains as a result of people acquiring and exercising power; in ideological and attitudinal change towards powerful people and institutions; and in mental health as a result of enhanced self-image.

To unravel the political nature of empowerment requires, as the first step, an examination of the assumption that there are groups of people in our society who have no power or who perceive themselves as powerless. A dialectical view of the nature of modern society argues that there is unequal distribution of power among various interest groups. The privileged classes who are the beneficiaries of the existing social arrangement try to preserve the *status quo* by exercising their power. Thus, in this analysis, powerlessness is a product of an oppressive social structure that sustains the power differential between the privileged classes and the powerless class. On the other hand, a structural: functional view attributes the problem to the erosion of mediating structures, such as the family, neighbourhood, and voluntary associations in modern society (Berger & Neuhaus, 1977). In this view, the individual is seen as powerless in the midst of the anonymous authority of government bureaucracies, economic institutions, professional groups, and policy planners. However, it is those who are most affected by public and welfare policies, and those who are the consumers of professional services, who are most vulnerable to this anonymous authority. They are the groups who feel powerless. They fall prey to unresponsive policies resulting from the separation of policy from practice, and the tide of managerialism that drives human service organisations as business organisations. Policies affecting the lives of those people who are most dependent on professional goods and services are made by policy-makers at the top, which are then implemented by professionals at the frontline. These policy-makers speak the language of economic rationalism. They are more concerned about efficiency, value for the dollar, and managerial accountability of the professionals implementing the policy. Clients, now often being referred to as users and consumers in the management language of service providers, are the ones at the delivery end, the ones who occupy the lowest position in the human service hierarchy. The notion of user involvement, or user control, has been coined by service providers to connote enlightened management. However, real power-sharing is hardly the case in so far as the final decision-making power is still preserved in the hands of policy-makers and administrators.

Given the above analysis, professional power is itself a significant element in empowerment practice. The issue is best captured by this question: What does it mean when social workers say "I am empowering people"? To empower others implies a power relationship between two parties whereby the party having power gives power to the other party who has less power, or enables the other party to acquire more power. Empowerment in this light implies the existence of a power differential between social workers and their clients. The latter may actually per-petuate the power differential in the professional: client relationship by conferring power to the professionals upon whose service they depend. On the other hand, power differential is inherent in the professional: client relationship (Weick, 1982; Hartman, 1993; Hasenfeld, 1987). Social work clients, as users of service, can make use of professional service only if they accept professional power. The power differential between professionals and their clients in modern societies is both ideological and psychological. It is ideological in that we are in an era of knowledge societies where power is controlled by knowledge groups. In the tradition of Foucault (1980), knowledge is power. Social work clients are in par-ticular a vulnerable group since they comprise the poor, the old, the dependent, the disabled, the deviant - the undervalued classes in modern societies

The Political Context: Past and Present

Hong Kong has been a British colony for almost 200 years. For a large part of the colony's history, perhaps until recent years, the political system has been charac-terised by an uneasy blending of freedom without democracy - if the latter means people having representation in the political process. Soon after the post-war years when a process of decolonisation took place in the Third World colonies, Hong Kong was nevertheless unaffected. The reason is that China has always maintained that Hong Kong is part of China and has made it clear that she will not tolerate any attempt to transform Hong Kong into an independent city-state. Neither has there been any strong expressed interest among the Chinese population in Hong Kong to seek independence. Unfortunately, any attempt to introduce greater participation of the people in the political process has been interpreted by China as a step towards a political landscape for the idea of independence to take hold. Indeed, the Sino-British dispute over the democratisation process in Hong Kong in the last few years has amply demonstrated the sensitivity of this issue.

A large sector of the Chinese population in Hong Kong has historically been excluded from the political power structure. There was some degree of political involvement among a small élite class of indigenous people - successful professionals, wealthy families enjoying a cosy relationship with the ruling class, business men controlling the local economy. This élite class was appointed by the Governor to serve as unofficial members in the Legislative Council, the law-making body in Hong Kong. In a study of these unofficial members of the Legislative Council for the period from 1948 to 1971 (Tang, 1973), the author concluded that the unofficial members over the years were and are either business men or business men with professional backgrounds (and) they were and are mostly those who hold leading positions - chairman or director - in these leading business corporations (p.199). Furthermore, they were a homogeneous group in terms of social and educational background, all from the upper strata of the society and also are the selected few of the government (Tang, 1973, p.201). Thus, the author concluded that the power structure in the colony is élitist in nature (p.202) and went on to question if such a monolithic power structure could still be maintained in the 70s as the society was becoming more pluralistic. He recommended that new channels for structural participation by the public must be opened up in order to maintain political integration and social stability. In fact, the Legislative Council has never been, and is still not, the most powerful body in the political system. The Executive Council has always been the power centre of government decision-making. Only a small élite group of insiders are appointed by the Governor as unofficial members of the Executive Council. The working of the Executive Council is opaque since its meetings are not open to the public. Its members are bound by the pledge to collective decision-making and the code of confidentiality such that there is always a semblance of political consensus.

Thus, until the democratisation process instituted after the signing of the Joint Sino-British Declaration in 1984, politics in Hong Kong had been essentially apolitical since the political system was basically administrative-driven under the exigencies of bureau-technocratic and fiscal considerations. In principle, the interest of the various groups in the élite class would have to be represented and balanced in government decision-making. However, the closed-door bargaining had never been accessible to the public. On the other hand, a façade of political participation was maintained through numerous consultative committees set up by the government whose members were appointed by the Governor. These consultative committees were given the mandate of putting up policy recommendations or proposing policy reviews. However, their resolutions did not have binding power on the government's decision-making.

In the public discourse, politics in Hong Kong has been framed under three overarching principles: economic rationalism, continuing prosperity, and stability. Economic consideration comes first in any public policy debate. The argument goes like this. It is essential that Hong Kong will continue to provide a stable social and political environment in order to attract foreign investment. Public policy is largely evaluated in terms of the economic cost (or economic efficiency) rather than the social cost. There is a collective belief (or myth?) that what is good for sustaining prosperity is good for the people, and what may seem to upset the *status quo* is a threat to stability which in turn will adversely affect the prosperity of Hong Kong. So goes a circular logic, and it works even in these days in providing the ideological ground for preserving the *status quo*.

Limited participation at the grass-roots level was first introduced by the government in the mid-70s in a three-tier system. At the lowest level is the Mutual Aid Committee (MAC), which was formed under the guidance of government officials to represent residents in a housing block. The original terms of reference for these MACs was to support government effort to fight crime and to keep Hong Kong clean by mobilising popular participation. At the middle level is the Area Committee (AC), which provided a forum for the representatives of MACs in a residential area, and human service agencies operating in that area, to discuss local issues affecting people's quality of life, such as environmental hygiene, transportation, law and order, and human service provisions. Officials in the MACs were elected by the residents. For the ACs, the government co-opted local business leaders, school principals and community agency administrators as appointed members. The last tier of grass-roots level participation is the District Board (DB), which was set up after the publication of the White Paper, The Future Development of Representative Government in Hong Kong (Hong Kong Government, 1984). This was the first major step taken by the government to galvanise grass-roots participation in the policy-making process, even though the authority of the DBs was still restricted to consultation. However, the DBs turned out to be a recruitment ground for grass-roots political leaders, and provided an arena for the first time for the common people to move policy issues onto the government agenda. What had started off as a political mechanism for absorbing grass-roots discontent and serving as the last rung in the ladder of consultative politics became, in recent years, the breeding ground of indigenous political leaders after Hong Kong entered into an era of party politics when direct election of the members of the Legislative Council was introduced in the White Paper, The Development of Representative Government: The Way Forward (Hong Kong Government, 1988). A system of consultative politics was being replaced by a system of representative politics.

The Biography of the People

People's political participation had been low, almost invisible, even as Hong Kong gradually transformed itself from a developing region to a developed region. Apart from the fact that the colonial system had discouraged political participation, people's attitude was another major factor. Indeed, one often-cited characteristic of Hong Kong people was that they were politically apathetic (Lau, 1982), were more concerned about self-interest than the public good and, true to the capitalist spirit which had rendered Hong Kong a good place to make quick money, were more concerned about having ends met and making more money. Herein lies the political wisdom, and a collective belief too, that people will be contented if economic prosperity was sustained, and law and order were maintained.

There is some degree of truth in such an argument for protecting the *status quo*. The population growth, which was phenomenal in the post-war years, was made up of a huge peasant class from southern China and a small group of intelligentsia and accomplished business men from central China. They fled to Hong Kong after the defeat of the Nationalists by the Communists in 1949, and in subsequent years as a result of widespread famine in the 50s and the Cultural Revolution in the 60s. Refugees who came in the 50s regarded Hong Kong as a temporary refuge, a borrowed time and a borrowed place. At first, they looked for a stable life and better material conditions, but what they had in mind was to accumulate some wealth such that they would be able to establish themselves once they returned to their native place when the worst was over. Politics was not their concern, and this was particularly true for the peasant class which was culturally conditioned to respect officialdom and to be subservient to authority. The mass political movements in the 50s till the mid-70s that racked China into decades of social, economic, and political turmoil had a clear lesson to tell to the population across the border - stay clear of politics.

Thus, despite an inefficient and corrupt bureaucracy in the 50s and 60s, the citizenry did not pose any demand on those who governed them. However, signs of discontent emerged among the younger generation in the late 60s and early 70s. First, what started as a peaceful sit-in protest to a five-cent rise in a ferry fare by a lone, young person was later transformed into a riot in 1966. This was the first sign of popular discontent. This was followed by an even more threatening leftist-incited riot in 1967 that disrupted law and order, and threatened to spread the Cultural Revolution to Hong Kong from across the border. In 1969, there was the Chinese Movement, which was a campaign to give Chinese language the status of official language (English was the official language despite the fact that English at that time was known only by the more privileged or educated people and that the population was over 98% Chinese). The Chinese Movement is a watershed event in that it marked the first sign of an activist student movement within the breeding ground of the power: ruling élite - the two local universities. Throughout the 70s till mid-80s, activist students projected a political profile of being leftist and/or populist. There was a wide spectrum of concerns among these activist students, ranging from the grand politics of Marx and Mao, to the local politics of campaigning against social injustice, to deeds of voluntarism and altruism. Many of these students were of the first local-born generation whose parents fled China in the 50s. They were much better educated than their parents, were receptive to western social and political thoughts, and at the same time were sceptical of traditional Chinese beliefs and values. After they left the universities, some remained loyal to the cause they had fought for in their student days and carried the torch on in various pressure groups. They were outside the institutionalised political system and yet sought to influence it. It was the result of their effort that pressure group politics and grass-root organising to develop a power base among the common people were added to the political landscape.

Another watershed event in the post-war political history of Hong Kong is the Sino-British Joint Declaration signed in 1984, which laid down a framework for the change of sovereignty by the end of June 1997. What had been a politically apathetic population became politically charged with the new awareness that politics was everybody's affair. At the same time, the government began to try at last to show its respect for the views of the people of Hong Kong. Abruptly, the people were pushed forward to the centre stage of Hong Kong's politics. Grass-roots participation in local politics was accelerated by the government-instituted political democratisation process. People exercised for the first time their political right of electing their representatives to the law-making body, the Legislative Council, in a dual-system of direct election and indirect election. What were formerly grass-roots pressure groups soon transformed themselves into coalitions espousing their brand of political ideology and special interest, and later on into rudimentary forms of political parties. At last, representative politics had replaced consultative politics, and the people of Hong Kong have a share of the political power by exercising their right to elect their representatives to the Legislative Council.

An Invisible Powerless Class
Throughout the 80s and up to the present, Hong Kong has enjoyed an extended period of continuous economic growth and relative affluence. The fruit of economic prosperity has trickled down to benefit a large cross-section of the population in the form of better housing, medical care, education, public transport

and, in short, improved quality of life. Unemployment has never been a serious threat to working class people except for the unfortunate few. Disposable income has increased to provide a broader margin of material comfort. There has been a growing middle class, too, with rising educational levels and a transforming economy requiring a more educated and better trained labour force. To a large sector of the citizenry, the *status quo* is therefore something to be preserved and hence the collective belief that what is important to the people of Hong Kong is stability and prosperity. As a silver lining, the process of political democratisation finally enables them to realise political participation in a system hitherto closed off from their reach. Now, they are entitled to elect their representatives to the Legislative Council.

However, economic growth and political democratisation had not benefited people in the lowest stratum of the society. The gap between the rich and the poor had actually increased. The Gini-coefficient was 0.45 in 1981 and increased to 0.48 in 1991; the income of the richest 20% of the population was 10.96 times the income of the bottom 20% in 1981 and the figure rose to 12.28 in 1991 (cited in Wong, 1993). These are the people who are most in need of social welfare, and who constitute the client population of social workers. They are old people with little money and living on their own, disabled people who cannot compete in an equitable manner in a capitalist society, the single mothers, the new immigrants from mainland China, the homeless. Ironically, the very success of contemporary Hong Kong has the effect of pushing them to the background as an invisible minority in an all-too-affluent society. They are the people who have to depend on social care, and therefore they are also most affected by the unresponsiveness of social policies and welfare practice.

The Social Welfare System in Hong Kong
The provision of social welfare is a public sector responsibility in Hong Kong. Welfare spending is basically borne by the government out of tax revenue. The guiding ideology that the government has adopted over the years in social welfare development is one that considers social welfare as a safety net for those sectors of the population who are most in need and yet who are least self-reliant. At the same time, government thinking has been dominated by economic rationalism. Social welfare is alleged to be a potential disincentive for people to work. Hence, cash assistance to the poor is available only to the most deserving. Furthermore, the level of support has been kept at bare subsistence level or else welfare recipients will lose the incentive to work. Social welfare provision is largely directed to the young, the old, the disabled, the deviant, and families with problems.

Social welfare is justified in terms of its remedial and restorative, and to some degree preventive, function as well. The control of welfare resource is in the hands of the government through a system of subvention which farms out funds to various NGOs who actually provide the services. The government has long been the lifeline of these NGOs since a large part of their operational budget draws on government subvention.

The development of social welfare policies has been in the hands of the policy-making branch of the Civil Service, supplemented by a system of consultation that comprises consultative committees, joint working parties between the Social Welfare Department and the Hong Kong Council of Social Service, and the issue of Green Papers (policy proposals) for public comment. The major actors in the policy process, other than government officials, are the administrators of the NGOs. The professional association of social workers, the Hong Kong Association of Social Workers, is at best a junior partner in the process.

The governance of the NGOs is in principle open to community control. The chief executive of these NGOs in most cases is a professional social worker who left direct practice in the early years of his/her professional life to take up administrative positions. The chief executive is accountable to a board of directors, or an executive committee, through which community control of these NGOs can be effected. However, on these agency boards, professionals, business men, and political élite are over-represented. There is a general absence of user representation in agency boards, except for a few rare cases. Thus, the client population has no involvement, not to say control, in the decision-making process that affects them most. It is curious that the process of political democratisation aimed at giving people their share of power in the political system has not been paralleled by an equivalent process of opening up social work agencies to user control. Why is it the case that a profession which emphasises the value of human agency and control fails to live up to its value in its own work? How can empowerment-based social work practice operate in an organisational context that disempowers their clients? Indeed, an even more basic question is: has there ever been an empowerment tradition in the local social work practice?

Empowerment in Community Work Practice
Social work in Hong Kong has its ideological root in western social work. There is a strong professional commitment to human agency, to the value of mastery and control, and to a rights-based ideology for the claim to welfare. In this light, there is a fertile ideological ground for empowerment practice to take hold in local

social work practice. Yet, empowerment has never, until recently, occupied a prominent position in the professional discourse of local social workers. In the past, professional discourse bearing a resemblance to the concept of empowerment was couched in such language as champion for the poor, enabling role, advocacy role, and helping clients to help themselves. The professional language portrays social workers as powerful agents in the society who are there to defend, to aid, and to rescue those people belonging to the undervalued and disadvantaged class.

Nevertheless, the mainstream of the social work community has been basically apolitical. This is true even in the case of community work practice which, by its very nature, should be the most political sector of all. Community work emerged in the 50s and, until the late 60s, had focused mainly on community development through self-help. Early efforts in community development work were under-taken by missionaries in rural areas with funds donated by philanthropic organisations in the developed countries. The aim of the community development effort was to improve health and community facilities, and to establish residents' co-operatives. Community work in urban areas first emerged in the late 60s and took the form of a pilot project undertaken by the Social Welfare Department in a resettlement housing estate. A U.N. consultant was brought in. The approach adopted in this project departed from the rural community development tradition. It took the form of organising at grass-roots level. Even though the project ended up sitting on the shelf, it marked the beginning of urban community work which became highly visible in the following decade.

One distinctive feature of urban community work in the 70s was its adherence to the Alinsky model of community organisation in the U.S. (Alinsky, 1969, 1972). It was the first time that social workers attracted media attention by their con-frontational posture and the conflict strategies they used as they fought on behalf of the poor and the oppressed. Community workers in those days inherited the language as well as the ideological outlook of the Alinsky model. In their view, the grass-roots people, or the mass, were powerless. They were the "have-not's", the oppressed class of an oppressive system perpetuated by a colonial regime serving the interest of the "have's" - big business and the élite class. Community organising was initiated by social workers seizing on issues that affected the livelihood of the grass-roots people. To begin with, these were issues of little sig-nificance to the *status quo*. Social workers entered into deprived communities - meaning in those days squatter areas, temporary housing, and resettlement housing - and organised local residents to press government officials for minor improvements in their living environment. The claims they tried to assert would seem trivial in these days - sanitation, lighting in communal spaces, and communal facilities. Nevertheless, it was through these small victories fighting these issues that grass-roots people educated themselves in the skills of taking collective action and sustaining the viability of the resident organisations they had developed.

Invariably, urban community organising in the 70s started off with an appeal to the self-interest of individuals and transformed it to a collective interest of people in similar circumstances - residents living in the same deprived neighbourhood and communities. Consciousness-raising was what social workers attempted among the residents in the early phase of organising work. Concerns about strategies and tactics dominated the professional discourse among community workers, and the conflict-consensus debate was a prevalent theme. However, and it was thought-provoking, professional discourse in this sector had never ventured beyond the question of strategies and tactics of community organising. Conspicuously absent was a structural analysis of the Hong Kong society which went beyond the rhetoric of the Alinsky model.

Has there been an empowerment tradition in community work practice in Hong Kong? We cannot answer this question until we have the answer to an even more fundamental question: What is empowerment? Earlier in this paper, it was noted that empowerment was a muddy concept. What matters here is not a question of definition. It is a question of the substantive content of the concept. In those days, the term "empowerment" did not appear in the discourse of community workers. Instead, "consciousness-raising" was the term used to denote what community workers did: the development of collective awareness among the grass-roots people of the nature of oppression, injustice, and mistreatment they were suffering; and of the potential for achieving change through community action as an organised group. Community workers at that time owed their ideo-logical roots to the work of Paulo Freire (1972), seeing consciousness-raising as having two components: the reflection in search of understanding dehumanising social structures, and the action aimed at altering societal conditions (Longres & McLeod, 1980). Government departments, which controlled resource-and policy-making, were invariably the target of community action. To the extent that community action by grass-roots people had been generally successful in gaining concessions from government departments, community workers over the last two decades might have already been empowering people who otherwise would not have the power or the action potential to improve their lives. In addition, the kind of issues being taken up by grass-roots organisations changed too. In the early years, people rallied around issues which were mostly local in character.

However, by the mid 80s, people became more vocal and aggressive in the public policy arena such as housing, public utilities, and labour. The picture was a rosy one - that of user involvement in public policy (Croft & Beresford, 1989).

Thus one could conclude that there has been an empowerment tradition in the community work practice in Hong Kong. If the essence of empowerment is to achieve power for those who are powerless, there were indeed many success stories of empowerment practice in community action projects. Grass-roots people formerly feeling powerless and with no access to power to improve their lot learnt the secret of gaining power – by organising themselves so as to acquire a power base and adopting conflict strategies to press for change. If this conclusion is warranted, empowerment may well be a redundant concept since the practice itself had existed before the concept of empowerment emerged. If what community workers in Hong Kong have been doing thus far has the effect of empowering people, what then is the point of substituting for an old concept (consciousness-raising) a new one (empowerment)?

Power in the Concept of Empowerment
Social work discourse on the concept of empowerment has been concerned with the normative aspect (as both the mission and the goal of social work intervention) and the action aspect (social work activities to empower people) of empowerment. What has been generally overlooked is the notion of power in the concept of empowerment. It is the conception of power that gives life to empowerment as a new concept to substitute for old ones, such as consciousness-raising. Power is a central notion in empowerment, it has been interpreted variously as giving power to the powerless, perceiving control, acquiring power, and using power. Consciousness-raising also embodies the notion of power since it too involves the politicisation of people (Longres & McCleod, 1980). It involves a process of helping people to acquire political literacy and, achieving that, to develop action potential for making change. But organising for power is taken for granted, and the notion of power is seen as unproblematic both in the process and as the end. Empowerment practice, however, puts the issue of power, including professional power, centre stage.

Given the power differential that is inherent in the professional relationship between social workers and the people they work with, and that professional education has socialised social workers to assume power and control, conscious-ness-raising may easily be turned into a teaching: learning process whereby social workers teach their clients the ideological perspective they wish the latter to adopt.

In turn, their clients would also encourage social workers to exercise professional power by virtue of their authority as professionals. Thus, social workers can dominate their clients even if they do not intend to do so. The term "conscious-ness-raising" itself may have misguided social workers to see it as an outcome of professional intervention. The action word "raising" people's consciousness suggests an active role on the part of the practitioner. There is also the implicit view that people either lack consciousness or have false consciousness. Thus, social workers who are ideologically committed would obviously be susceptible to the temptation of selling their ideological perspective to their clients - and this may well have been the case. Community action projects in the past were mostly concerned with public issues (such as housing) but not private troubles (such as marital disharmony), and demonstrated a propensity to regard government departments as the target of community action. Moreover, community workers often looked for group consensus in an ideological standpoint among the partici-pants in community action projects.

If this is a fair observation, community workers in Hong Kong may have succeeded in giving power to the powerless, but they are not empowering them. Indeed, social workers who try to supply an ideology to the people, who want to empower them with their professional power to liberate, who see their profes-sional role as the catalyst, the teacher, the strategist, the enabler, may turn out to be disempowering their clients. When that is the case, empowerment takes place to the extent allocated by those (social workers in the present discussion) with power (and) inequity continues to exist (Hess, 1984, p.230). Therein lies the paradox of empowerment - a basic contradiction in the idea of people empower-ing others because the very institutional structure that puts one group in a position to empower also works to undermine the act of empowerment (Gruber and Trickett, 1987; cited in Simon, 1990, p.32). How can social workers empower their clients if not by what they do? How can their clients perceive themselves as having power if that power would not have been theirs without the initial action of social workers? Indeed, the very idea of professional interven-tion is antithetical to the concept of empowerment. If empowerment is the goal of professional intervention, social workers will then be empowering people by what they do, and at the same time will also be disempowering these people by their professional power to liberate. As social workers we may unwittingly and well meaningly disempower our clients through our role as expert, through the authority of our knowledge (Hartman, 1992, p.483).

Community action projects can be disempowering in yet another way when the goal is to help people gain power and to use that power in advancing their self-interest, even if there is a morally justifiable claim to that self-interest. The language of strategies and tactics - in the Alinsky tradition - turns power into power-play. Inadvertently, community workers have advocated a one-dimensional view of power, seeing power as domination, as power over an adversary. Implicit is the view that power was some finite phenomenon always in limited supply and that being powerful involved an assertion of control and strength over others (Rees, 1991, p.46). People organise themselves to acquire power, and the power acquired may then be exercised to coerce the powerful - and to oppress the less powerful as well. Sadly, we witnessed in recent years several instances of community actions in which resident groups exercised their power to shunt facilities and services for the mentally disabled out of their community. They are the people who are being described as poor and powerless (and) were being oppressed by the rich and powerful élite (Cheung, 1990, p.209). Yet having empowered themselves, they turn their power onto the less powerful. Is there an apparent paradox between the emphasis on community care on the one hand and the promotion of community empowerment on the other? (p.210). Yes, this is going to be the case if empowerment practice continues to reinforce a one-dimensional view of power and to assume a morality of collective self-interest.

Rees (1991) is right to rejuvenate a morally defensible interpretation of power - that of power as potency. It is the power to achieve goals which are liberating for others and which provide a sense of self-enhancing creativity for the actor or actors (p.15). Power is exercised to achieve a moral end - which is not self-interest, even if it is the self-interest of a community, but justice and equity, and the promotion of the interest of the most vulnerable groups in a population. A truly empowering practice in community work will also require its practitioners to demystify their claims to professional power founded on their professional expertise. The process of empowerment begins with political literacy which involves clients reflecting on their biographical situation in relation to the social order and appreciating how wider forces constrain lives by rendering people powerless to comprehend, make challenges or develop alternatives (Rees, 1991, p.12). This cannot be achieved by treating people as clients, as the object of professional intervention, or as consumers of professional service. It is through dialogue that people unravel in each other's stories the political in the personal, and start to act in association with others to achieve justice and equity that affect their lives as well as others'. Social workers' claim to professional expertise actually hampers this process by reinforcing professional control and the image of clients as consumers of professional service. Instead, empowerment practice requires social workers to achieve some sense of equality and partnership in their relationship with the people they work with by recognising that each party can lay claim to expertise by learning from the other (Rees, 1991, p.71).

Beyond Casework:
Advocacy/Empowerment Practice in Family Service Settings
The concept of empowerment finds its expression at the personal level when people perceive control over their lives. However, empowerment practice has often been seen as a form of macro-practice, and therefore falls within the province of community workers. One would expect that this concept has little meaning to social workers in family service settings. Family service is one of those services long established in Hong Kong. It is also the service where profes-sionalisation of its work force has the longest history. Casework is the staple method of practice among family service workers although the generalist orienta-tion has been adopted by local social work educators over the last decade. Indeed, practice in family service settings is still dominated by a clinical-therapeutic ori-entation. In addition, clinical practice has long been seen as more professional than most other forms of practice by local social workers. Professionalism is expressed in the clinical language that practitioners use to talk about their work. They practise "brand-name" therapies and are intent on learning more. Family service agencies reinforce such a professional culture by emphasising the use of theory in practice. A number of these agencies have actually institutionalised theory-driven practice by requiring their social workers to identify explicitly the particular theoretical approach they use in a case.

It is therefore unexpected that there are family service workers who espouse a conception of practice beyond the confines of the clinical-therapeutic orientation of casework practice. In an exploratory study of practitioners' notions of good practice, I conducted a focused group interview with three practitioners who worked in the same family service centre of a large social welfare agency. The two women in the group, Irene and Yin-ming, were experienced social workers, having worked in the family service division of the agency for more than eight years. The male worker, Koo, was new to the agency. Previously, he had partic-ipated in youth work for four years. The interview started off with the question: How would you perceive the term "good practice"? A few minutes into the dis-cussion, Irene shared her observation of the constraints imposed on caseworkers in their day-to-day work. What follows is extracted from the written record of the interview prepared by me:

She (Irene) found that caseworkers were often being restricted to giving direct service to individual cases. They were either too absorbed in working with individual clients to the point that they were oblivious to societal changes, or so exhausted that they had little energy for performing the advocacy role even if it would mean sacrificing their clients' needs. She lamented that it was not just the clients feeling powerless. Social workers too were beset by the sense of powerlessness. However, in her view, advocacy should be the right direction to pursue. If social workers were happy with the *status quo*, there would be no policy change. The more social workers tried to get their clients to accept the *status quo*, the more they would feel powerless. . . .

Koo echoed Irene's sense of frustration. Unlike community workers, family service workers were much less "macro" in perspective. They were handicapped in addressing issues in the policy plane . . . family service workers were locked in case-level work. How could they respond to the changes around them?

She (Yin-ming) thought that a social worker, after practising for a period of time, would come to recognise that many of her clients' problems were actually problems of the broader system. . . . Previously, practice was confined to casework and the focus was to work with individual cases. In these days, practice should be more comprehensive and thus would require social workers to see things in a broader plane.

She (Irene) recognised the limit on caseworkers. Heavy workload rendered it almost impossible for workers to go beyond individual casework unless there was agency support. There was a discrepancy between what practitioners considered as "good practice" and what agencies would like to do. The latter were more preoccupied with giving service at the case level. (Later on) she acknowledged that accountability was something of concern to the agency. If social workers put too much time into the advocacy role, it would affect direct service.

It would not be uncommon that other social workers did not consider it the job of family service workers to rock the boat. Other members of the professional community would think that advocacy should be the job of those activist groups. Such attitudes in their professional peers rendered their feeling of powerlessness even stronger. They were confined to working at the case level and could not elevate their work to a higher (systems) level. It is such constraints that breed discontent among family service workers.

What they can do is to share their clients' feelings, but they are not allowed to move beyond such confines.

To family service workers, frustration was in store for them, and exhaustion too. Not just the worker but the client, too, had that sense of being trapped. In their social work training, they were told to accept limitations, and they asked their clients to accept limitations too. But the emergent trend is to find a solution, not ventilation. She (Irene) acknowledged that we could still find good practice even if we only looked into the casework process (that is, case-level work). However, she thought that we would have to look beyond the case level to achieve "good practice". This was her reasoning: what happened at the macro-level would affect our work at case level, and would determine whether our work was effective. It makes no sense at all to keep providing casework service to a client over long years, probably from one generation to another, trapping them in the client role all the time.

Here, we are listening to the voice of three social workers about their work in a family service centre. They did not like the way their work was being defined and then imposed on them. It was casework all right, but it was a form of practice that trapped their clients, and themselves too, within an oppressive system. They recognised that private troubles were essentially public issues. They would like to have influence on social policies, and yet they were not supposed to do so, nor did they have the room for going beyond case-level work. It was a disempowering experience. Their voices may have conveyed a feeling of despair and powerlessness, yet they had something hopeful in store. Later on in the interview, they talked about professional growth, learning and change, in order that one was able to look at things in a broader plane. They talked about a new approach which in fact is a version of empowerment practice at case-level work.

(the new approach) is that the client solves her problem, not the worker. In this way, the client will have enhanced confidence in herself, instead of having confidence in the worker. (Irene then contrasted this to the professionally instituted client role.) Whenever a client came to see a social worker, she would be expected to tell her problem. The client role is to talk about problems, and such role definition is reinforced by the worker. So even if the client has been seeing the worker for long years, she is still led to believe that the worker is right and she is wrong. Thus, it is the social workers who keep their clients having problems.

It is not clear whether the voice of these three social workers is also the voice of many more social workers practising in family service settings. Probably their experience is also the experience of many social workers. After all, social workers will not miss the point that the personal becomes political when many clients tell the same story about their problems. Yet, there is very little that family service workers can do unless their employing agencies are ready to enlarge the clinical-therapeutic orientation to include advocacy/empowerment in their definition of what constitutes service to their clients. Such flexibility will not be easy to come by if accountability is still translated into the number of cases that a social worker and, for that matter, an agency processes. None the less, change may well be in sight. In the same interview, these three family service workers, cited a recent development of their agency. Noting that there were many cases about an extramarital affair, the agency tried to respond to this phenomenon by developing preventive work in this area, and drawing public attention to it. At the same time, the agency developed other service responses beyond case-level work, such as mutual aid groups and self-help networks. This is empowerment practice. As Rose (1990) puts it, the primary focus of advocacy/empowerment practice is to develop consciousness and active participation in shaping one's life through creating and shaping networks of social support and action and the political is very intimately personal as well (p51).

The Future of Empowerment Practice in Social Work
An over-used concept, which is used loosely, will soon lose its vitality. This may well be the case for the concept of empowerment. Social work literature in the West has been flooded with this concept, to the extent that whatever the claim of empowerment practice it has no substantive meaning. Probably, this is also what is happening here in Hong Kong. Practitioners use this concept to characterise what they do, but it is not clear if they are indeed referring to a concept or using newly popular jargon. I recall a tutorial session with a group of practising social workers who are studying part-time in our programme. I asked these students to examine the professional language that they used to talk about their practice. A student came up with the word "empowerment" and he was a community worker. He told me that this concept surfaced about two years ago. However, when I asked him if the emergence of it resulted in a change in practice he replied "No" and that his way of work was still the same. To him, the concept was synonymous with consciousness-raising.

Unless social workers are serious about the professional language they use, a potentially powerful new concept will lose its meaning. Empowerment, as argued in this paper, puts the centrality of power in social work practice and, indeed, in our conduct of social life, under sharp focus. Empowerment practice in community work entails reframing of the professional role and requires social workers to rethink the nature of professional expertise in their practice. To adopt the philosophy of empowerment, social workers should not impose their expertise, but instead should use their expertise as a tool for empowerment within the context of an equal partnership with their clients (Hess, 1984). Seeing themselves as the organiser of community action, and seeing the people they work with as the oppressed class, community workers will need self-discipline and self-awareness to resist the temptation of seeking to organise the people to change the system or to demand better treatment. Even more important is that they need to rethink their notion of power, which in the past was power over other people. They have yet to find out what it means to see power as potency and what this interpretation of power will mean to their practice.

Rethinking professional power in the context of empowerment practice, it is clear that our claim to professional knowledge actually hampers empowerment practice. Instead, social workers must continually factor in local knowledge (Simon, 1990, p.36) and lend support to the "insurrection of subjugated knowledge" of our clients (Hartman, 1992). The new awakening is meaningful to social workers in every field of practice, and those in casework practice in particular. Furthermore, casework practice will be too confining for those family service workers who are attracted to the philosophy of empowerment. Empowerment practice in casework goes beyond casework as well as the confines of the traditional definition of family service.

In closing, it is important to emphasise once again that there is a new concept for the social work profession in Hong Kong. The opportunity may be missed once more if we, as members of the professional community, are uncritical of its meaning.

References:

Alinsky, S. D. (1969) *Reveille for Radicals.* New York: Vintage Books.

Alinksy, S. D. (1972) *Rules for Radicals.* New York: Vintage Books.

Berger, P. L. & Neuhaus, R. J. (1977) *To Empower People: The Role of Mediating Structures in Public Policy.* Washington, D.C.: American Enterprise Institute for Public Policy Research.

Cheung, F. M. (1990) People Against the Mentally Ill: Community Opposition to Residential Treatment Facilities. *Community Mental Health Journal,* Vol. 26 (2), pp 205-212.

Croft, S. & Beresford, P. (1989) User-involvement, Citizenship and Social Policy. *Critical Social Policy,* Vol. 9 (20), pp.5-18.

Foucault, M. (1980) *Power/Knowledge.* Ed. C. Gorden; trans. C; Gordon, L; Marshall, J; Mepham and K. Soper. New York: Pantheon Books.

Freire, P. (1972) *Pedagogy of the Oppressed.* Harmondsworth: Penguin.

Hartman, A. (1992) In Search of Subjugated Knowledge. *Social Work,* Vol. 37 (6), pp.483-484.

Hartman, A. (1993) The Professional is Political. *Social Work,* Vol. 38 (4), 365-66, 504.

Hasenfeld, Y. (1987) Power in Social Work Practice. *Social Service Review*, Vol. 61 (3), pp.469-483.

Hess, R. (1984) Thought in Empowerment. In J. Rappaport, C. Swift & R. Hess (Eds.) *Studies in Empowerment*. New York: Haworth.

Hong Kong Government (1984) *White Paper: The Future Development of Representative Government in Hong Kong*. Hong Kong: Government Printer.

Hong Kong Government (1988) White Paper: *The Development of Representative Government: The Way Forward*. Hong Kong: Government Printer.

Kieffer, C. H. (1984) Citizen Empowerment: A Developmental Perspective. In J. Rappaport, C. Swift & R. Hess (Eds.) *Studies in Empowerment*. New York: Haworth.

Lau, S. K. (1982) *Society and Politics in Hong Kong*. Hong Kong: The Chinese University Press.

Longres, J. F. & McLeod, E. (1980) Consciousness Raising and Social Work Practice. *Social Casework*, Vol. 61 (5), pp. 267-276.

Midgley, J. (1981) *Professional Imperialism: Social Work in the Third World*. London: Heinemann.

Rappaport, J. (1987) Terms of Empowerment/Exemplars of Prevention: Toward a Theory of Community Psychology. *American Journal of Community Psychology*, Vol. 15 (2), pp. 121-148.

Rees, S. (1991) *Achieving Power: Practice and Policy in Social Welfare*. St Leonards, NSW, Australia: Allen & Unwin.

Rose, S. M. (1990) Advocacy/Empowerment: An Approach to Clinical Practice for Social Work. *Journal of Sociology and Social Welfare*, Vol. 17 (2), pp.41-51.

Simon, B. L. (1990) Rethinking Empowerment. *Journal of Progressive Human Services*, Vol. 1 (1),pp. 27-39.

Solomon, B. B. (1976) *Black Empowerment: Social Work in Oppressed Communities*. New York: Columbia University Press.

Tang, L. W. (1973) *The Power Structure in a Colonial Society - A Sociological Study of the Unofficial Members of the Legislative Council in Hong Kong (1948 - 1971)*. A Senior Thesis submitted in partial satisfaction of the requirement for the degree Bachelor of Soc. Sc. in Sociology, the Chinese University of Hong Kong.

Weick, A. (1982) Issues of Power in Social Work Practice. In A. Weick & S. Vandiver (Eds.) *Women, Power, and Change*. Washington, D.C.: NASW.

Wong, C. K. (1993) *Social Work and Social Change: A Profile of the Activist Social Workers in Hong Kong*. Hong Kong: Hong Kong Institute of Asia-Pacific Studies, the Chinese University of Hong Kong.

Part II
Pathways to empowering the oppressed

Empowering Women:
The Women's Development Centre in Gyumri

Ludmila Harutunian and Rose Rachman

Summary

This chapter describes the way in which members of the educational part-nership between theArmenian National Academy and London School of Economics worked with women in Gyumri in the Republic of Armenia, many of whose children were killed in the 1988 earthquake. We consider how engaging with the women who perceive themselves as "like spiders in a bottle" can begin to empower them to believe they can exert influence and make changes in their lives. We reflect upon issues arising from this experi-ence and the dilemmas this poses for social work practice.

"The tragedy of Armenia starts with the genocide in 1915, continues with the earthquake in 1926, and all those years from 1937 and again in 1947 when the intelligentsia were deported by Stalin. I thought for two years after the earth-quake, the Soviets could restore life, but now I know that is not possible. The old system has collapsed like the houses. Life is without rules. There is no law and order. No respect, no system of state protection. We have a great problem of reconstruction now and of adaptation to the new economy. Our psychology has changed; in Gyumri we used to be like a family, a small close circle. Now everybody is different. We are like spiders in a glass bottle. I am powerless and cannot struggle against my fate."

"For me, the greatest tragedy is the earthquake here in Gyumri in 1988 when I lost my daughter. She was just 23. The Institute collapsed - it was a seven-storey building; 85 young people were killed. In Gyumri, everything stopped then, the clocks stopped, the houses, the schools, the factories and the old church fell down - all just piles of stones with the people buried beneath them for many days." (Interviews with Women of Gyumri 1995.)

This earthquake in 1988 was the worst to occur in the Caucasus for the past 80 years and the worst in Soviet history. Leninakan, as Gyumri was then known, a prosperous and commercial city, was devastated by this natural disaster. Many thousands were killed, injured and left permanently disabled. Factories, business-es, schools, and houses collapsed in piles of rubble, leaving thousands homeless and unemployed. By any analysis of world disasters this was a harrowing catalogue of death, damage and dislocation.

The ensuing social, economic and political changes which have accompanied the dissolution of the Soviet Union and the subsequent energy crisis have resulted in appalling social conditions, large scale unemployment and inadequate housing.

Gyumri has become a town predominantly of women, older men and children. Many of the younger men have left the town and even the country in search of work. With few factories and an irregular supply of power, there is little opportunity for employment. The town has many problems, but it is the women of Gyumri who are in the greatest need of assistance.

Powerless people are without influence or energy to be active on their own behalf. Most women in socialist countries, disempowered by the tight social control exercised by the State, had become accustomed to allowing others to make decisions for them. Lack of participation reinforced their dependency. Unable to effect changes, many women passively accepted their situation. As in Gyumri, this affects the social functioning of individuals, groups and communities. The powerlessness that we are concerned with here is that of both individuals and a community. As a result of cumulative multiple adversities, neither individuals nor the community have been able to obtain the resources which would allow them to take advantage of life's chances.

Traditionally, the activity of helping powerless people to overcome personal or social disadvantages has been the domain of social work in the West. Fundamental to good practice is the need to empower those who are powerless and disadvantaged by a lack of available resources. We began with the premise that the women of Gyumri are equal citizens, rather than passive recipients of professional decisions. As facilitators and educationists, our role was to encourage participation and partnership in the process and promote active citizenship for the collective benefit (Biehal 1993).

The central focus of this chapter is on participation by and empowerment of women, which by its very nature must be about restoring power to the powerless. It incorporates a notion of active citizenship to maximise opportunities for women to exercise choice in shaping their lives (Einhorn 1991).

In this chapter we consider whether it is possible for women who perceive themselves to be "like spiders in a bottle" to believe that they can exert influence and make changes in their life situation. We discuss whether citizens, who have had little experience of participation in local affairs, can begin to gain control over their lives in a town devastated by geographical, ecological, political and economic disasters.

This is a study of empowerment which takes the form of helping the women of Gyumri to initiate a centre as a support system for women who were unable to achieve individual or collective goals. Empowerment is both a process and a goal. Empowering people enables them to become active agents of their own fate, motivated to effect change in their life situation. Fundamental to the process is the need for participation in making decisions in order to exert influence and bring situations under one's control.

Empowerment as a process: explorations and discussions
Our involvement in Gyumri arose at the end of a three-year collaborative educational programme to assist in the development of social work in Armenia, initiated by Shula Ramon at the London School of Economics and funded by the Soros Foundation. We describe the process by which we engaged with the women of Gyumri in locating the problem and deciding what steps needed to be taken in promoting the idea of a centre for the women. We reflect upon issues arising from this experience and the dilemmas this poses for social work practice.

First impressions
In April 1994, when the authors first visited Gyumri, we met the newly elected Mayor and his council, who said that although the town had many problems, it was the women of Gyumri who were in greatest need of assistance. The biggest problems were structural: the lack of housing, employment and money. The men had left the town in search of work and the women were without work. Many organisations were providing aid. Food parcels, kerosene and building materials for repairing the containers were being dispensed by the newly created Social Services Department. The Department of Pensions dealt with benefits now grossly eroded by inflation. Citizens had access to the Mayor, which ensured they were heard, even if nothing much could be done.

Initially, the Mayor thought more humanitarian aid was needed, but agreed this would only be a short term solution. Since the earthquake, the town had received considerable financial assistance, but every week the numbers of people needing aid seemed to increase. As we explored the issues, it was clear that the reconstruction programmes by local and central government had been ineffective, for the problems were not responsive to financial aid alone.

People were apathetic. Tested almost to the limit of their endurance, they had little desire to make any changes in their life situations. Part of the apathy related to living in dreadful circumstances, which removed hope that something could be done and that it could be achieved by their own actions. Under the former system of government, citizens were not expected to take control of their lives and were not rewarded for initiative.

For the majority of the population, before the reforms life had been politically and economically stable. Under socialism, a well-ordered, structured system of social control regulated the lives of the citizens. Universal employment, despite low wages and low productivity, and a system of benefits and pensions ensured economic security. The family was under the protection of the State which provided a network of child-care institutions, benefits and allowances and community services. As the State looked after the people, there were no officially recognised social problems.

The collapse of socialism has radically altered the view held about the role and functions of the State. As one woman council member said: "Gyumri has changed. There is no system now . . . no system of protection. We have to create new connections, a new life for ourselves."

Life in Gyumri is completely different now. Despite aid from the West, Armenia is in a parlous state. Gyumri in particular has been hard hit. Once a prosperous town, its industry has been brought almost to a standstill. There is no development in the public transport system. The physical infrastructure has all but collapsed. Roads, railways, buses and trains are in poor condition with little possibility of repairs being effected. The building programme has all but stopped and the workers have returned to Russia, leaving less than 15% of housing units and less than 7% of nursery schools completed (Poghosyan 1990).

In addition, the conversion to a market economy, raging inflation, the introduction of its own currency and the instability of the dram have left the population struggling to survive. People are simply unable to manage financially. Even those who regarded themselves as well provided for now find that, due to the disintegration of the economy, the value of savings, pensions and benefits has been eroded. Armenians are a proud people and dislike being dependent on charity. For the people of Gyumri, accustomed to being hospitable, this is especially hard.

Recognising that we would be unable to provide financial aid or contribute to the housing programme, we began to explore ways of helping the women to reestablish a system of child care facilities, for, even if they could find work, women were unable to work unless their children were cared for.

Creating new connections
As a first step, we needed to know more about Gyumri, the effect of the earthquake and how women were perceived in their society. We also needed to know if

the women of the town shared the same view of both the problem and the solution. We needed more information on how to begin to create groups for women in the community to work for change. This process of finding out would empower both of us as strangers to the community. Sharing our knowledge and observations with them would enable the women to think about their needs and how these might best be met.

Learning about Armenia from the women and the literature
Talking to the women, it was apparent that they bore the brunt of the economic crisis. It was primarily they who struggled to maintain their families despite the erratic power and water supplies, shortages of food and lack of goods and household appliances. Many of the women spoke of their shame in having to go to the Mayor or the Social Services for assistance, but they had no where else to turn.

Armenian women say they have yet to be liberated. Even before the collapse of socialism, it was recognised that women were the real proletariats of the Soviet Union. Although the provision of paid work and an occupation was a major component of Soviet policy for liberating women, in reality occupational trends show significant inequalities. Women's education and employment were skewed, so that despite 40% of women holding degrees, only 7% were represented in managerial jobs. There is considerable evidence of discrimination against women in positions of authority and political power, where they occupied supporting rather than leading roles.

Since the dissolution, fewer women than before are in any positions of power. Even well-educated Armenian women pointed out that they occupied the poorest - paid jobs in textiles, medicine, teaching, culture and shop management. This is a situation common to other states of eastern central Europe. In Armenia by 1991, 60% of those whom the market forces made redundant were women (Lane 1992).

Weighed down by family responsibilities, few women in Armenia see themselves as having any position of power or influence outside the family home. Family roles are very clearly delineated. Men's sphere of influence is in the world of work, government and politics; women are responsible for the maintenance of the family, the care of children and of elderly relatives. Although there are child care facilities, it is usual for women who have small children to care for them themselves. Even working women expect to deal with all the household and family responsibilities. Numerous surveys in the former Soviet Union suggest that there have been no significant changes in the woman's role within the family, and that women with an occupation still carry the main burden of child care.

Families support and sustain each other. They present a closed and united front to strangers or external threats. Armenians follow a patriarchal system with the newly married woman moving into the home of her husband's family. Traditionally the extended family live together and comprise three generations – grandparents, married son and daughter-in-law and their children. Unmarried girls live in the parental home until marriage. Great respect is accorded to older people in the family. Fathers are the head of the family: they represent family members externally, make the decisions, choose the bride. Mothers reign over domestic matters, instruct the daughter-in-law and care for the children. Rural families have always followed these customs; but within the last 15-20 years, people in towns have begun to move away from these traditions, with younger people choosing their partners and living separately. Now, due to the difficult conditions and because they are unable to live separately, families are returning to traditional ways.

The old Gyumri
In Gyumri, the women are proud of their traditions. They tell you: "We have many customs and culture. You cannot compare the new town with the old town. You have to know about how we used to live, to understand how we live now. We understand we have to do things for ourselves, but people think now only of keeping their own family, without thinking of the neighbours. Before, we thought about our neighbours, we thought about our work, our family, our community."

Gyumri, the second largest city of Soviet Armenia, is an ancient town. Its fortunes, which had declined under the Turkish-Persian regime, later revived and by 1897, with a population of 32,000, it was the third most important Transcaucasian town. It had a well-developed educational system: as the birthplace of the Revolutionary movement which was to create the future Soviet society, it prided itself on its intelligentsia and educated professional people.

Although not a capital city, it had a highly developed cultural life. Many musicians, artists, sculptors and writers of national and international significance lived and worked in Gyumri. It had a thriving economy and was a most prosperous and commercial town. People enjoyed a good standard of living, were hard-working and took great satisfaction in the level of their achievements. They said, "we, the people of Gyumri, have a special character - we are warm, we laugh, we have a big heart, we are more generous than people from Yerevan".

Resurgence of nationalism
Like most Armenians, people in Gyumri are fiercely nationalistic. The distinctive national and ethnic consciousness has been reinforced by the Church, which remains the cultural and emotional heart of the nation. It survived the Communist

regime, and many would suggest is the vessel of Armenian language, culture and national cohesion.

The continuing political and military conflict with Azerbaijan, the war in the Karabakh (an Armenian enclave in Azerbaijan), and the massacre of 31 Armenians in Sumgait have only served to strengthen nationalism. There is strong support for the inclusion of the Nagorno-Karabakh.

The women tell you they have endured centuries of war. They tell you with pride how neither wars nor earthquakes will make them leave their land. They have lost many of their men in the struggles and have a collective memory of disasters and tragedy. They ask if you have heard about the massacre on 24th April 1915 in which one and a half million Armenians were killed by the Turks; and the earthquake of 22nd October 1926 which destroyed 40% of the buildings, killed 400 people and made 50,000 homeless. They mourn their dead. Even at the time of the earthquake and Gorbachev's visit to Gyumri, people were clamouring for the return of the Karabakh and reminded him of the victims of the war as well as those of the earthquake.

The "Spitak" earthquake
On 7th December 1988 at 11.41am an earthquake measuring 6.9 on the Richter scale struck Soviet Transcausia devastating Armenia's northern region. Two-thirds of Gyumri were destroyed; Spitak was reported to be the hardest hit with tens of thousands killed and buildings razed to the ground; half of Kirovokan was toppled and tremors were felt as far west as Baku in Azerbaijan and north in Tbilisi in Georgia. Unlike Chernobyl, the earthquake disaster was fully reported by the national and international press. Official figures recorded 25,000 dead, 12,000 injured and 400,000 made homeless.

The people of the towns put the figure much higher. Almost everyone in Gyumri experienced a loss; for some this was close family members, for others distant relatives, colleagues or neighbours. The Mayor of Gyumri lost 15 members of his family. Many more thousands were injured and left with a permanent disability. The disruption to life affected the whole community.

Gyumri was described as looking like "a scene from a war film". Newspapers carried heart-rending pictures of the women of Gyumri mourning their lost relatives, homeless and destitute, facing sub-zero temperatures and waiting in the street to reclaim the bodies. Faulty construction led to the collapse of new, prefabricated nine-storey buildings. Schools, hospitals, factories, housing estates fell apart like houses of cards.

73

The Soviet Union willingly accepted aid and praised the world-wide response to the plight of the Armenians. Specialist teams of rescue workers, doctors, and medical supplies were flown in. There was an urgent need for temporary shelter, blankets, clothing and supplies which were co-ordinated by the Soviet Red Cross. Gorbachev promised immediate help to feed and shelter survivors, medical aid, and said the town would be rebuilt in two years.

Five days after the disaster, hundreds of people were still climbing over the debris tugging with bare hands at chunks of concrete, steel girders and splintered timbers. Gradually the teams began to withdraw. Tent cities were erected for refugees. As the last survivors were being pulled out of the wreckage, the focus turned to the reconstruction of their lives.

Ecological and political disasters
Since 1987 events in the Soviet Union have impacted upon Armenia. The nuclear disaster at Chernobyl in April 1986 and the earthquake in 1988 alerted the Armenian National Party to the potential environmental hazards which they faced. Concern at the level of pollution led to closure of several factories. After the earthquake, the nuclear power station at Metsamor, situated on a geological fault line, was shut down. The newly elected government's hopes to be able to rely on alternative sources of power from neighbouring countries were short-lived. The Republic faced an unprecedented energy crisis in the winter of 1991-2, when Azerbaijan cut the gas supply line crossing its territory and stopped rail traffic.

Knowledge about collective action
Given all this, where to start? It was easy to understand how overwhelming the scale of disasters must seem to people in Gyumri. When consulting colleagues involved in women's movements and co-operative groups, we were comforted to know that others had trod this path before us in other countries. The most important thing we were told was that organisations start with an idea: "... wouldn't it be a good idea if ...?" Working out the idea is the next stage. But too many good ideas were lost if this took too long. Energy was dissipated, enthusiasm and motivation waned, and nothing happened. We were urged that whatever project we agreed upon with the members who would determine the goal, it must be realistic and achievable.

It was clear the women of Gyumri were in need of assistance. What form that would take would depend on them. Our task was to ensure it was possible, to equip ourselves with the knowledge they would need, to secure some funding to ensure we could begin and "start small". But above all, to start.

Returning to Gyumri

We returned to Gyumri for three weeks in August 1994, and spoke to many women about their experiences over the past six years. We also met with representatives of local and central government, the institute of education, non-government organisations, banks and commerce. We attended the weekly drop-in surgery held by the mayor and listened to the stories of those who approached him for assistance in dealing with their problems. We observed a similar surgery held twice weekly by the Principal of the newly created Social Services. We wanted to know what the women saw as problems that needed intervention, and how they had been managing. We needed to find out what the official response was, what developments were being proposed, but most of all what it was possible to achieve.

Problems facing the women

Almost all the women had suffered losses during the earthquake: children, parents, husbands, sisters and brothers, friends or neighbours. Many were struggling to care for their families and themselves under the most difficult circumstances. They were fearful of the approaching winter and had little hope that things would get better. Others, who had escaped without personal tragedy, had lost their homes and possessions, their factories and employment. Many young women, who six years ago were the casualties of the large-scale destruction of the schools and institutes, have been left with physical injuries and are permanently disabled.

Conditions in Gyumri are appalling. Many buildings, needing to be destroyed, are still standing - a daily reminder to people of the earthquake. People who had been living in prefabricated temporary shelters - known as containers or dormics - now face little prospect of being rehoused. Winters are severe, the containers, poorly insulated and in need of repair, offer inadequate protection against the weather. Families are having to bring up their children in dreadful circumstances with little possibility of any immediate improvement.

People in the towns complain of a serious shortage of basic food supplies. Bread and milk are rationed. Despite having been issued with cards for bread, people still have to spend considerable time in queues. Material assistance from the West, given in the form of food parcels, is creating a culture of dependency. As they face their sixth winter after the earthquake, families are tired of struggling for survival. They urgently need food, kerosene, building materials; but above all they need hope.

Of all the deprivations, they found the irregular and infrequent supply of power the most difficult. Without electricity they could not cook, without water they could not keep their homes, family and themselves clean. And yet, despite all this, every day they were out and about on the streets, carefully dressed, well made up and above all cheerful. Obviously not everybody has recovered - many women, traumatised by the earthquake, are still in mourning and are very distressed.

Gyumri women say they are strong. They have no alternative now. They are proud of how their parents survived the earlier disasters, but say the conditions under which they are living are even worse. They speak of the challenges which they are facing and the ways in which they are dealing with them. Some are learning new skills and are taking courses; others are beginning to write about their experiences, yet others continue to do handiwork – mostly by candlelight. Armenian women are known for their fine embroidery, sewing and knitting skills. They encourage each other by saying "we must do something, no matter how small". They need to believe that life can be different and that they can make it so.

All were having difficulty in managing, but some had not only developed strategies for coping but were creative, actively managing their situation, and engaged in the process of reconstruction. In reflecting upon what it is that makes some people less vulnerable to life's disasters, we have identified that it is those women who have a resilience and a perseverance; have well-established social supports and close personal relationships, who are able to use the changing social, economic and political conditions to foster new opportunities for growth and development.

Starting small: The Women's Development Centre
The women were interested in the idea of a centre. Initially this was seen as a meeting place to discuss their difficulties, but as people continued to develop the idea, they wanted something more than that. They wanted to do something concrete that would have an impact on their lives. They were proud of their handiwork and thought they could bring this to the centre. We were to try and find a market for their work. Many were interested in the notion of "food for work", and thought they could get extra food parcels for their family if they did engage in some community work, either at the centre or in the town. Women thought this would restore some of their dignity and pride and made suggestions as to the form of work that could be undertaken - visiting the sick, looking after children, selling their work, repairing toys and clothes for recycling, organising a toy/clothes exchange shop, a drop-in café and cooking food for this. Someone thought the centre should have a hairdresser and the disabled women began to talk about a place where they could learn new skills. People were excited and enthusiastic, brought examples of their work, and began to extend the idea.

Discussions were held with people with influential positions, the Mayor, the Governor of the Shirac region, the Rektor of the Institute of Education, the Principal of the Social Services. The Centre was approved by the City Council and supported by the Mayor who offered rent-free premises. It was agreed that initially the centre would be sited in the building of the social services, because many of the women who are in need come there for food parcels. The bank agreed to provide all the necessary banking services, facilities and financial advice. A small grant has enabled the Centre to apply for registration, open a bank account and begin a women's newspaper.

Discussions were held with enterprising women in the town, who have been attempting individually to tackle problems of unemployment and child care, by establishing kindergartens, creating work for the disabled, setting up small factories, and developing the cultural centre. They recognised the need for collaboration and formed a Council of Women which would support and extend the Centre. We were asked to provide consultation, seek support and funding.

"Think big . . ."
We met with representatives of non-government agencies who were interested in the idea. People recognised the limitations of financial aid and wanted to support developmental projects. Initially we asked for a small pump-priming sum. We were encouraged, as one colleague said, "to think big. Don't restrict yourself before you have even begun". We began to submit proposals for funding and have now secured money for a retraining service for the disabled women who will learn new skills. We have been able to attract funding for education and research from the London School of Economics. One project has just begun in which graduate psychology students from Gyumri will receive university-based training in social work and will do three-month practice placements in Gyumri and in the Centre. We have three more projects in mind – a women's press and monthly community newspaper; promoting women's health; and child care facilities.

Issues and dilemmas: empowerment is not a "soft option"
For empowerment to be both a process and a goal, workers and participants need to view themselves as equal partners in the interaction, bounded by rights and responsibilities to each other and to their wider communities. Social workers have different theoretical perspectives underpinning their practice which have led them to work with the "disadvantaged" as individuals, groups or as a community. Each has validity, but the choice of perspective has implications for practice in dealing with the inequalities inherent in the roles of help-seeker and help-giver. Whilst not denying the value of more-traditional therapeutic approaches, we

support developing a model of intervention in which the strengths are built upon to develop a service for those in the community who are without social supports. We invite workers to consider both professionals and participants as experts in their own fields. Each is a resource for the other and brings knowledge, skills, values and much life experience to the interaction. Viewing the participants as the experts in knowing what they need leads social workers towards a model based on facilitation. Workers are a resource for participants to use to meet their expressed needs. Such an approach raises questions about equality in the partnership.

Partnerships are not equal

For social workers in the West, partnerships pose a dilemma. Constrained by the functions of their agencies, or the legal framework which sanctions their practice, or both, workers are only too aware of the inequality of the partnership, and the disempowering nature of their interventions. Even in situations which do not call for the exercise of statutory powers, workers can facilitate or restrict access to resources.

Equally, the process of receiving help can be disempowering to those whose rights are already circumscribed by structural factors. Practitioners, when asked, would say they involved users of services as partners, but in reality this was not always so. Good and inventive practice does exist, but more needs to be done to achieve greater partnership with users (Marsh and Fisher 1992).

Underpinning the concepts of partnership and participation in decision-making is the notion of users as equal and active citizens (Beresford and Croft 1986). Applying this to the former Soviet Union poses a dilemma. In Gyumri, many people who have suffered such cumulative deprivation over the past six years are apathetic, unwilling and unaccustomed to such participation. Yet, the need for participation is greater, for it encourages confidence and develops co-operation: the more people become involved in their local community the better.

In addition, the system of tight social control which existed in former socialist states militated against making decisions and taking the initiative. The process is further complicated by the additional authority which is accorded to foreigners. Some of the women who were articulate, active and involved in their community wanted us, rather than them, to meet with those in powerful positions because we would be listened to and they would not.

In a society where women are not accustomed to being in authority, outside of their carefully ascribed role within the family, they have no experience of being consulted about determining their needs. People are hesitant to enter into partnerships with authority figures, particularly if they have known them in positions of power before the reforms.

We were told by many women how much they had wanted to talk about their suffering. They talked to each other, and to officials, but had not felt heard. As one said, "we want to talk and we want people to listen. It is the best help of all. We want a supportive service, but not one from these officials".

Autonomy and self-determination

Empowerment is not an easy process. It challenges professionals to put into practice the core values of social work; respect for the person and the right to self-determination. Social work is about helping people and communities to resolve intransigent personal and social problems. The debate in practice has been how to enable people to be self-determining, whether defined as freedom from coercion or the fulfilment of potential within the restrictions imposed by society and the law.

In holding firm to these values, one has to believe that people do know what they want and have a right to expect to be able to get it. But that is self-determination at its simplest level; it omits the conflict where these needs are at the expense of others; where attainment is impossible; bound to fail; or in direct opposition to the values of society. Social workers may have to hold the balance and in doing so exercise power, which will conflict with personal and professional values. Acknowledgement of the power vested by the legal framework and derived from societal values is difficult, but a necessary part of the interaction. Everyone is powerless in some way where limitations are imposed upon their self-determination. The way in which power is exercised when difficult decisions have to be made lies at the heart of skilful and sensitive practice. Power can be used to enhance people's lives as when used by social workers to protect the most vulnerable in society from being further disadvantaged. The core dilemma of the protection versus autonomy debate is about assessment of risk (Stevenson and Parsloe 1993).

In conclusion

We began by considering how best to help powerless people to overcome personal and social disadvantage exacerbated by political and economic instability. Clearly structural problems require solutions beyond the scope of this project, but giving the women of Gyumri a voice to express their needs and to believe that they can influence events are the first step. As one woman said, "I have to say nobody came to speak to us before. Nobody asked us how we felt. Nobody wanted to know about our sorrows. I feel very good now that I have spoken to you. I feel easier, I feel stronger".

Talking gave them strength and was the first step to moving forward. One woman wrote to us after we had visited to say: "The terrible earthquake took from me my two loving children and at the same time my life. All these years I feel that I am not living. The endless pain and sorrow wrung out of me and I live like a robot.

It seems to me that this society does not need me and I think all the time about committing suicide. After your visit, during those days, I felt many changes inside me as if I am again a person. The pressing heaviness became a little bit easier. It seems to me that my lost hope is restored."

We asked the women of Gyumri how they saw the future. Many still preoccupied with grief saw no hope, but others spoke of having had to accommodate themselves to their losses. All were proud of their strength at being able to stand the pain and suffering. Older women had hopes of living to see their children and families survive, they wanted things to be different, but were uncertain of their ability to create those changes. Younger women saw it differently – "we are the future, we have to believe, we are the builders, not all of us think this way but we want changes. We don't mind changes. We think change is an opportunity. We are afraid we may not live up to it and we need people to help us to do this".

Helping women create a centre will provide them with a formal support network, which will strengthen existing social relationships, create new ones, and provide a forum through which the women can organise collectively and so help secure their own future and that of their children. As such, it is also concerned with the social, economic and political advancement of the women and not just their immediate problems.

References

Beresford, P. and Croft, S. (1986) *Whose Welfare?* Brighton, Lewis Cohen Urban Studies Centre

Biehal, N. (1993) "Changing Practice: Participation, Rights and Community Care" in *British Journal of Social Work* 23, 443-458

Einhorn, B. (1991) *Cinderall goes to Market.* London, Verso

Lane, D. (1992) *Soviet Society under Perestroika* London, Routledge

Marsh, P. and Fisher, M. (1992) *Good Intentions.* York, Joseph Rowntree Foundation with Community Care

Poghosyan, H. (1990) "The process of construction and reconstruction in the disaster zone" *International Bulletin for the Reconstruction and Development of Armenia,* 2, 1-3

Stevenson, O. and Parsloe, P. (1993) *Community Care and Empowerment.* York, Joseph Rowntree Foundation

Times Newspapers. December 8-12, 1988. London

Old People and Empowerment:
The Position of Old People in Contemporary British Society

Olive Stevenson

Summary

This chapter provides an appraisal of the position of old people in contemporary British society, drawing out the factors such as ageism and sexism and a rapidly changing society which must be acknowledged when attempts are made to empower them. The need to balance autonomy and protection and to recognise the possibility of abuse are noted, as is the position of carers and the implications of resource constraints. Finally, the importance of interpersonal processes between old people and those who work with them and the possibility of empowerment in the small choices of everyday life is stressed.

This chapter addresses the issue of empowerment in relation to the work which social services, and social workers in particular, undertake with old people. Empowerment has, of course, much wider political resonances. It is used here only to describe a way of working with individuals and families where the needs of old people are the focus of attention. The underlying principle, however, remains the same – to shift the balance of power between the parties. Particular importance is attached to the notion of empowerment as a process as well as a goal. Without detailed consideration of the details of the process of empowerment, the goal can become mere rhetoric.

The discussion which follows is based upon an appraisal of the position of old people in contemporary British society and draws upon knowledge of the work of social services which, in Britain, has been mainly concentrated within the statutory sector of local government. The extent to which this will change, with current political preference for increased use of the independent sector, private and voluntary, is as yet unclear and will not be debated here. In any case, it does not affect the fundamental thrust of the argument that radical change is needed in society, specifically by officials and professionals, in the attitudes towards, and value ascribed to, old people.

There is now widespread acceptance that "ageism" in our society is pervasive. By "ageism", we mean derogatory attitudes, "feelings such as contempt of the young and strong for the old and weak, fear of the mortality which old age represents..."

(Norman, 1987, p.3) which may lead us to turn away from old people. It has been a sociological truism that ours has been a youth-centred culture in which physical strength and youthful beauty are deified and powerfully reinforced by the media. At the same time, however, demographic trends in all western countries show an increase relatively and absolutely in the numbers of old people, mainly due to the reduction in mortality in earlier years; particularly striking is the increase in numbers of very old people, with whom this chapter is mainly concerned. These are facts that cannot be ignored by citizens in their daily experience, which often involves providing care, by professionals, notably doctors and nurses, whose work is increasingly focused upon old people and by politicians whose awareness has been raised of the voting power of elderly people.

A large majority of very old people are women. This introduces a further complication in social attitudes in which sexism as well as ageism plays a part. Indeed, as the present author has shown elsewhere (Stevenson, 1986) there are sinister and ugly feelings and fears specifically about old women. These matters cannot be explored here but they form a background to the discussion of empowerment. For they suggest that there are powerful forces, internally and externally, working against our efforts to accord old people, especially women, the dignity and respect due to them.

In addition to an acknowledgement of these negative attitudes, we have to recognise that various factors make problematic the status of very old people in contemporary society. First, there is the fact that disability rises steeply amongst those over 70 or 75. This is a phenomenon described by doctors as 'compressed morbidity'; that is to say, most elderly people over retirement age live healthy and active lives until the last decade or two of life. We have learnt how to keep people alive but not how to combat successfully disability and associated health problems at the end of their lives.

Secondly, we have what might be described as an "existential" problem relating to the social integration of elderly people into society. At any period of rapid social change when traditional modes of activity undergo transformation, the contribution of older people to the functioning of society may be undermined. Knowledge and skills related to earlier activities may no longer be valued and older people may feel uneasy with contemporary trends. The technological revolution of the late twentieth century is a case in point. There is a sub-committee of the European Commission on Science and Technology (COST A5) which specifically addresses the question of older people and their use of technology. It is apparent from the work undertaken that whilst there is tremendous potential in technological applications for the well-being of older people, there is a pressing need for a more sensitive and informed understanding of old people's fears and anxieties about their utilisation. Of even more fundamental concern is very old people's doubt about what they have to contribute to modern society. If traditional knowledge and skill are no longer relevant, and we are surrounded by bewilderingly complex technology, what do very old people have to give, especially since so many have serious disability with which to contend, which limits social involvement? Thus the search for purpose and meaning in life in later years is a preoccupation, often expressed in simpler terms, by very old people, who do not want their last years to be centred solely on taking or receiving from others. There is, of course, the elusive concept of "wisdom", of a combination of knowledge and experience which transcends ordinary practical contributions to the lives of others. Whilst it is not difficult to cite examples of "wise" old persons, we are less than honest if we gloss over the fact that many younger people do not experience older people as having wisdom to impart. Part of this may be due to ageism but part of it reflects a real problem in defining the areas in which the older person can make a significant impact.

These are issues which have to be addressed by those who provide services, if they wish to engage in a process of empowerment. It is likely that a significant number of those (many) old people who suffer from depression, are depressed because they perceive (with reality) their lives as lacking purpose and meaning, often compounded by isolation. (In Great Britain, a very high proportion of very old people [women] live alone.) This is not a clinical but an ontological problem.

Any account of the position of very old people in contemporary British society would be incomplete without reference to the numbers (probably about 1 in 4 of over 80s) who suffer from dementia or other serious mental infirmity. Such people will be over-represented in those whom social workers seek to help, since, inevitably, their vulnerability makes them a target for intervention. We shall return to this group in considering processes related to empowerment.

The picture painted above may seem bleak, but without a clear view of the characteristics and problems of the group of old people with whom social workers are likely to work, realistic discussion of empowerment is impossible. Clearly, this picture is not of old people as a whole. "Young" old people, generally, and those well able to support themselves do not generally come the way of social workers.

Autonomy and protection
Amongst those who need social work help, an issue crucial to empowerment is the balance to be struck between autonomy and protection. The objective of empowerment is to move the individual towards maximum possible autonomy, that is, to the greatest possible degree of personal responsibility for decisions and actions in

their lives. It is now widely recognised that officials and professionals may undermine autonomy - whether intentionally or not – by the ways in which they work with people. For example, withholding, selective, or inadequate sharing of information may restrict choice.

More subtly, "taking charge" of planning for people, even when exercised with benign intent, can undermine confidence and, in the case of old people, erode long-established patterns of independence.

The case for autonomy is based on a strongly held belief, enshrined in the law, that adults, unlike children, are "competent" beings, whose right to make decisions about their own lives is rarely challenged, provided they conform with the general norms and values of society. Indeed, there is even a degree of licence accorded to elderly people, whose deviations may be regarded as eccentric rather than dangerous!

In keeping with general trends in British social work, those involved in promoting the ideal of empowerment amongst old people stress the significance of autonomy and the need to work towards achieving this in greater measure amongst their clientele. However, it is essential that such ideals are integrated with the reality of the need for protection of some old people, vulnerable because of disability, mental or physical, and also simply because of frailty associated with very old age. In practice, British social workers are likely to be involved in service provision when there is deemed to be "risk", physical, emotional, or even financial, to particular old people.

The question of "risk" is complicated. Who says there is "risk"? What kind of risk? Who is worried?

Physical frailty and disability increase environmental risk, both inside and outside the home. In particular, falls are extremely common. The nature of the injury and shock sustained frequently have long-standing effects on mobility and confidence in the very old. Clearly, therefore, it is in the interests of old people that hazards are reduced. Similarly, the onset of dementia creates a situation – often spanning a number of years - in which an old person takes "risks" at home which society finds unacceptable. For example, the risk of fire or flood, burning or scalding, is frequent in such cases. Nor is the risk limited to the old person him or herself since their action or inaction may place in danger those who live near them.

Attention is increasingly being drawn to the risk of abuse by others. This has been a neglected area (in contrast to the field of child welfare) but there is no doubt that a significant, if small, proportion of old people are abused, physically and even sexually, by those who supposedly "care" for them whether in the family or in institutional settings. Local government social services and local health authorities are now in the process of drawing up policy and procedural guidelines for their staff to deal more effectively with referral, investigation and intervention.

There is also mounting concern that many old people are subjected to financial abuse; at its grossest, this may involve coercion by relatives to part with the house owned by the old person; less serious, but of concern, is the "pocketing" of State benefits paid to old persons. Emotional abuse is difficult to define but social workers not infrequently encounter situations in which an old person feels intimidated and harassed even when there is no direct physical abuse.

Such are the day to day experiences of social workers who work in this field. They cannot ignore issues of "risk" and "abuse". Yet they must constantly bear in mind the "competence" of old persons to make choices and decisions for themselves. If an old person refuses help and thereby places himself or herself at risk, what is the responsibility of the social worker? In what circumstances would the wishes of the old person be overruled? What legal framework for such intervention is required?

These matters have been the subject of discussion by the English Law Commission which has produced a valuable consultation document in "Mentally Incapacitated and other Vulnerable Adults" (HMSO, 1993). The Commission attempted to define the circumstances under which the protective functions of the state should be brought into play. The key elements in their proposals are that:

any action taken should be "in the best interests" of the incapacitated person, taking into account:

(a) the ascertainable past and present wishes and feelings of the incapacitated person;

(b) the need to encourage and permit the incapacitated person to participate in any decision making to the fullest extent of which he or she is capable;

(c) the general principle that the course least restrictive of the incapacitated persons freedom of decision and action is likely to be in his or her best interests (Law Commission HMSO, 1993, p.75).

An incapacitated person may be one suffering from mental disorder as presently defined in British legislation; or a person who is vulnerable by reason of old age, infirmity or disability if he or she is unable to take care of himself or herself or to protect him or herself from others. (pp.77/78).

Although there are difficulties in deciding what may be in a client's "best interests", the Law Commission have suggested safeguards which go a long way to prevent the arbitrary use of power by the professionals. This document, then, represents a very real attempt to balance the concepts of autonomy and protection. Most important of all, it could reduce the likelihood of old people being "tidied away" into residential care against their wishes unless it is clearly demonstrated that they are seriously mentally incapacitated. However, the present state of British law and policy does not enable these proposals to be put into practice and leaves social workers in an invidious position.

There is one aspect of empowering practice with old people which distinguishes it from most work with other client/user groups. It is inevitable that some old people face a progressive decline in autonomy over a period of years. Indeed, some are willing to relinquish a significant degree of autonomy for protection and are willing to give up responsibility. Some very old people are, quite simply, tired of shouldering all the tasks of daily living. Others fight all the way, despite increasing difficulty and disability. The onset of increasing dependence, whether sudden or gradual, is characterised by ambivalence. It is essential that social workers recognise and work with that ambivalence, recognising the struggle which is going on and seeking to preserve autonomy in those domains of life most valued by the individuals concerned.

The position of carers
Although the main focus of this chapter is upon very old people, we also need to address the role of the social worker in those situations in which informal carers occupy a pivotal place in the support of the old person.

In the past decade or so, we have seen in Britain the rise of what may be described as a "carers movement" and the development of an active national organisation advocating on their behalf. Social workers have become much more aware of the burden and stress carried by those who provide care for old people, whether in the same household or not. Although carers are not a heterogenous group and include a significant number of elderly spouses, men and women, caring for each other, it is generally agreed that when care is provided by younger people, especially when it takes the form of physical and practical assistance, it is usually women who bear the brunt. Many of those women are "young elderly" and many are unaccustomed to seek help from formal services. Their feelings and needs have been well articulated, mainly by feminist writers (see for example: Finch and Groves, 1983; Qureshi and Walker, 1988; Lewis and Meredith, 1989) and this has drawn attention to the disempowering experiences which may be associated with the caring role. This may be because the carers need for support and help is not adequately met by statutory agencies but the problem is more deeply rooted than that. There are some situations in which the carer becomes progressively more isolated, locked into a pattern of home care in which the social world contracts and emotional life becomes intensely and narrowly focused on the relationship with the old person. This is likely to be particularly damaging when the old person suffers from dementia; many carers comment that they have "lost the person whom they knew"; reciprocity in relationship is no longer possible and any communication may become unrewarding. The effect of this on the self-esteem of the carer is very negative. Furthermore, this kind of stress may in some cases lead to abuse of the old person, when patience is exhausted. Social workers must therefore address issues of empowerment in relation to carers. Recent government guidance, following community care legislation, requires a separate assessment of carers' needs from that accorded to the old person. Many social workers are now actively engaged in fostering carers' groups whose objectives include self-advocacy for more support, practical, emotional and financial.

However, I have explored elsewhere (Parsloe and Stevenson, 1993) the complexity of the position of carers *vis-à-vis* old people and the difficulties which the social worker must seek to resolve in working with both. I have suggested that social workers have tended "to side with" carers rather than old people, whereas in other areas, such as work with younger, disabled people, social workers have empathised more readily with the user/client. It seems likely that this reflects ageist attitudes and a degree of insensitivity to feelings which the old person may have about a process of care in which they may feel progressively "disempowered" as dependency increases. However that may be, social workers often have to face situations in which there is a degree of conflict between the needs and wishes of the two parties. Sometimes, the task is to achieve a balance between the two; sometimes the conflict may be irreconcilable, most commonly when the burden and strain on the carer are such that admission of the old person to residential care is inevitable but is not in accord with the wishes of the old person.

In many spheres of their activity, social workers are required to manage conflict and the ambivalence which this raises in them. This is less often discussed in adult care than in child welfare but is just as challenging and complex. Honesty about these situations is an essential prerequisite to empowering work.

Resource constraints
Thus far, I have concentrated upon those situations, often of great complexity, in which ideals of empowerment are necessarily modified by the incapacity of the old person and by conflict of interest between carer and old person. Sadly, however, other factors impede the implementation of the ideal. These centre upon

resource constraints under which social workers currently operate. Some of these constraints reflect general deficits in social security and social service provision, deficits which are disempowering in themselves. If many old people are poor, relative to others in the population; if their access to health care for non-life-threatening surgery is seriously delayed; if their housing is unsuitable, even unsafe, and remedial action or alternative housing is not readily available; if public transport is unsuitable or unavailable – the effect is to diminish their quality of life and to reinforce deep feelings of stigma, the very opposite of empowerment. In Britain today, there are old people who are relatively prosperous, thanks usually to occupational pensions. But there are a very large number living in, or on the margins of, poverty with all the associated deprivations referred to above. These are the people with whom social workers are most likely to be in touch. Their valuable role as advocates and supporters of old people who need to challenge "the system", to obtain increased benefits or better housing, for example, should not be overlooked. Indeed, social work in the West has its roots in a response to poverty and disadvantage and it cannot abdicate its responsibilities when the going gets tough. None the less, one must acknowledge that "disempowering factors" are frequently outside the sphere of influence of the social workers.

At the present time, British social workers are seeking to implement policies of community care. By far the greatest numbers of those in need of service are elderly. Old people consume by far the greatest share of the personal social services cake. The policy underpinning community care is unequivocal. In a remarkable statement in a policy document, it was asserted:

> *"The rationale for this reorganisation is the empowerment of users and carers. Instead of users and carers being subordinate to the wishes of service providers, the roles will be progressively adjusted. In this way users and carers will be enabled to exercise the same power as consumers of other services."*

(Department of Health Practitioners Guide, 1991.)

As a general statement of principle, this is welcomed and endorsed by British social workers. Many, however, are perplexed and troubled by the discrepancy between policy and practice brought about by serious resource deficiencies within their own services. Such deficiencies, they argue, make real choice – the existence of options - difficult if not impossible and "choice" is integral to empowerment. Thus, for example, the choice to stay at home or move into residential care is not a meaningful one if the home and personal care services to facilitate staying at home are not available; or if there is no choice between residential establishments, the decision being dictated by cost or availability rather than the needs and wishes of the old person. British social workers, therefore, are well aware that the ideal of empowerment could be discredited by the inadequacy of provision.

Whilst it is important to acknowledge the context in which British social workers currently operate, there is a danger that such difficulties may be used to deflect attention from the interpersonal processes which are also crucial to empowerment by social workers. Old people are no strangers to hardship, shortages and poverty. They know more about this than younger people! Many of their needs and requests are moderate, even minimal. Their feelings and attitudes, however, are much affected by the manner in which their requests are handled. For example, in a small study undertaken by a voluntary agency, old people were angry and depressed when they did not hear about the outcome of their application in a reasonable time or were not informed of its progress. This left them feeling disempowered. More generally, the care taken in discussing needs and wishes, the respect and concern which are shown, leave a profound impression. To translate that into effective communication requires skill and empathy. Pacing of conversation and adaptation to deafness are two seemingly simple examples. More complex, and very important, is the work needed to communicate effectively with those who have a degree of dementia. Even when intellect is failing, and rational discussion difficult, trust and confidence can be established by a social worker who is in tune with the underlying feelings of the person. It should be remembered that, in paying attention to the details of daily living, which are so important to elderly people, it may be possible to offer choice, to facilitate empowerment in matters, seemingly trivial, which in fact effect a sense of comfort and well-being. Thus, the days of the week when a day of home care services is offered, the achievement of minor housing repairs, the organisation of shopping which takes account of preferences for this kind of food rather than another, the delivery of ethnically appropriate meals – all this and much more is a symbol of taking old people's needs and wishes seriously. The social worker is not, of course, the provider of all such help. Many other people may be involved. However, a key role in social service provision is that of a "care manager", who may be a social worker, and whose role is to assess need with the old person concerned and to ensure integration and sensitivity in the care provided. Thus a vital element in empowerment by care managers is the part which they play and the example which they give in ensuring that others provide service which is in tune with the old person's wishes, which is not demeaning and which leaves the old person reassured that they have some control over what might be described as their "daily destinies".

Thus far it has been emphasised that the role of the social worker involves assessment of need which can itself be empowering by the manner in which it is conducted and attempting to influence the way services are offered and provided to maximise choice, even in minor matters.

Face-to-face work
There remains at the heart of the process a simple, yet infinitely complex, concept of seeking to understand, to empathise with the old person. For there is ample evidence that the experience of another person trying to understand one's perspective and one's situation is in itself empowering. It is a symbol of respect. Now that it is more easily said that done. Social workers have not reached that stage of life and its associated feelings and difficulties. Bereavement, for example, is a less-common experience for younger people. Feelings about dying are less-prominent – often pushed away. If this lack of old age experience is combined with ageist attitudes referred to at the beginning of this chapter, which may be shown in patronising or condescending behaviour, it is very easy for the encounter between worker and old person to be disempowering for the latter.

In recent years there has been an emphasis on the need to encourage elderly people to assert their rights. Reference has been to "grey power", to the increasing politicisation of older people. Most of this has come from the USA and there is little evidence of such organised movements in Britain although the existence of a group of elderly people with significant purchasing and voting power has a social impact. However, they are not the groups with which social workers most often come into contact. The very old (who are, by and large, also poorer) do not readily form coalitions and effective groupings – for very obvious reasons. For the foreseeable future, empowering work with such people will usually take place at an individual or familial level. It requires a fundamental change of attitudes by many social workers, who will need to examine their feelings and views about ageing and old age, and an application of the empowerment ideal to this group of clients. It will also require a concentration on skills of communication appropriate to these situations. The foundations of good practice are laid, well illustrated in traditional casework literature. What is needed is to build on these foundations, acknowledging the new emphasis in shifting the balance of power and the extent to which old people have been neglected in the process.

References

Department of Health, (1991) *Practitioners Guide.* HMSO.

Finch, J. and Groves, D. (1983) *A labour of love: Women, Work and Caring.* Routledge Kegan Paul.

Lewis, J. and Meredith, B. (1989) *Daughters who Care.* Routledge Kegan Paul.

Norman, A. (1987) *Aspects of Ageism.* Centre for Policy on Ageing.

Parsloe, P. and Stevenson, O. (1993) *Community Care and Empowerment* Rowntree Foundation.

Qureshi, H. and Walker, A. (1988) *The Caring Relationship.* Routledge Kegan Paul.

Stevenson, O. (1986) *Women in Old Age: reflections on policy and practice.* Nottingham University.

The Law Commission, (1993) *Mentally Incapacitated and other Vulnerable Adults. HMSO.*

Work with Families where Children are at Risk: Control and/or Empowerment?

Margaret Boushel and Elaine Farmer

Summary

In this chapter we shall examine the extent to which imbalances of power between families and the State, as well as those within families, have been understood and dealt with in social work practice. Concentrating on developments in Britain, we shall examine how views of abuse of or harm to children have changed over time, the situations in which State interventions in family life are most likely to arise, and the types of intervention currently in use. We shall then consider a framework for policy and practice that seeks to build on the strengths of children and their families, and to acknowledge the difficulties and disadvantages they may experience. Using this framework, we shall consider how social workers and policy-makers might develop an approach to practice that is both safe for children and empowering for them and their parents.

How Views of Risk to Children have Changed Over Time

Social work with children and families is not a neutral activity. At any one time child care practice will be affected by competing values about the responsibility of the State to protect children and the autonomy of the family. Nowhere is this more evident than in work with families where children are at risk of abuse or neglect (Dingwall *et al.* 1983, Parton 1985). Not only do social and political forces shape the way in which services respond to children in difficulty and children at risk, but they also shape the way in which we recognise and understand what constitutes child abuse itself (Gordon 1989).

British history illustrates how views of risk to children change and develop over time. Before the 1870s, government intervention to protect children was rudimentary and dealt only with orphaned and homeless children and young offenders. It was motivated by a concern to protect society *from* children. In Behlmer's view:

"To patrol industry on behalf of the young was England's sacred duty. To patrol the home was a sacrilege" (Behlmer 1982).

However, fuelled by an evangelical Christian zeal to rescue children, a turning point was reached in 1889 when the Prevention of Cruelty to Children Act was passed. This Act, for the first time, enabled courts to remove children from cruel parents.

The major concerns of the time were about physical abuse, and to a lesser extent sexual abuse (Parker *in* Farmer and Owen 1995).

After the 1914 - 1918 war the issue of child abuse almost disappeared from the public agenda. There were repeated claims that physical cruelty was no longer the problem it had been. Where neglect was discovered it was seen as due to the short-comings of mothers. By the 1960s the child care issue which caused most concern was delinquency. Again it was seen as arising from children neglected as a result of poor mothering.

In the UK the 'rediscovery' of child abuse, and specifically physical abuse, had to await the death of a seven-year-old child. Maria Colwell died in 1973 at the hands of her stepfather. Her death attracted enormous attention from the media, and the social workers who had returned her home at the request of her family were blamed for failing to protect her. This re-emergence of a recognition of physical abuse (previously called cruelty) followed in the wake of the work of Henry Kempe and his colleagues in the United States. Kempe published an influential paper about 'baby battering' in 1962, drawing on evidence provided by new radiological tech-niques which made it easier to detect injuries sustained by children. He and his colleagues attributed such injuries to deliberate mistreatment on the part of parents (Kempe *et al*.1962).

The nature of British public concern shifted again in the late 1980s, following a government-funded public inquiry called the Cleveland Inquiry. This investigated the situation in one local area in Britain, Cleveland, where an unprecedented number of children (again with the aid of a new diagnostic technique) had been diagnosed as having been sexually abused and removed from the care of their parents (Secretary of State 1988). The sexual abuse of children, often by a family member, re-emerged as a major cause for concern after having disappeared from sight for virtually a century.

The increasing recognition of sexual abuse was accompanied by a renewed media attack on social workers. Previously they had been criticised for doing too little too late. Now they came in for criticism for having done too much too soon, that is, for removing too many children from their parents on too little evidence. The publicity surrounding the Cleveland Inquiry yet again dramatically exposed a long-standing dilemma in child protection. How could the tension between taking action to protect children who might be at risk plus respecting their rights and those of their parents best be managed?

As we have seen, during different periods of British history different kinds of harm to children have become the focus of public concern, but throughout there are also certain consistencies as to what is taken to merit attention. In particular, it is evident that most effort is made to protect children from family members and to protect society from delinquent children. Very much less effort is expended on trying to improve the circumstances which most profoundly affect children's development, such as poverty, poor housing and poor education. This is in spite of the fact that 'child poverty has been rising relentlessly in the UK since 1979 and, by 1991, it was affecting nearly one in every three children' (Kumar 1993, p1). This suggests a preference for a model of State intervention to protect children in which certain individuals are singled out for attention rather than a more structural view of the way in which some children are consistently disadvantaged by government policies which ensure that financial support, education and health care are unequally distributed among the total population (Baldwin and Spencer 1993).

Which Children at Risk Receive Most Services?

At the present time in the UK, children who are at risk from family members as a result of physical abuse, neglect or sexual abuse are given priority by social work services. Rather fewer resources are available for helping adolescents who may be at risk as a result of their own behaviour, such as young people who sniff glue, take drugs or break the law.

In fact, recent legislative changes have reduced the financial support, training and housing options available to school-leavers (Coffield *et al.* 1986) and this, in turn, has led directly to a sharp increase in homelessness amongst this age group, with accompanying problems of drug and alcohol dependency, prostitution and petty crime. These young people are very much at risk, but most of them receive no statutory social work service because of their age. It is worrying that a considerable proportion of these young people had previously been known to social work services because, following family breakdown or child abuse, they had lived away from their families in residential or foster care.

Work with Families with Children at Risk

Given that children who are at risk of abuse and neglect within their families are given priority, what kind of services do they receive? Work with these children has developed in a distinctive way in the UK. Influenced by the outcry over Maria Colwell's death, the UK government has laid down a set of procedures for identifying children at risk of abuse or neglect from family members and co-ordinating good professional help to assess and protect them. Adherence to procedures is intended to protect vulnerable children but it is also relied on by social workers to spread responsibility for the decisions made among a group of professionals and so protect themselves from public censure if a child should come to any harm.

A spate of public inquiries into the deaths of other children has ensured that child abuse has remained high on the public agenda (DHSS 1982, Department of Health 1991). Professional shortcomings have frequently been highlighted and the child protection procedures successively revised.

There are three main elements in the procedures in the UK which are intended to improve inter-agency communication in the handling of child abuse. Since 1974 the local authorities, who employ social workers to undertake child protection work, have been expected, first, to form area committees (now Area Child Protection Committees) to oversee local policy and training arrangements; second, to ensure that case conferences which bring together a range of professionals are held following every suspected case of child abuse or neglect; and third, to set up a central record of information or list of all children believed to be at risk (now called the child protection register). It is central to the operation of the child protection system that children at risk are reliably identified and swift action is taken to protect them. Protective action may involve placing children's names on the child protection register so that the children can be supervised at home by social workers and other professionals and expectations placed on parents to improve their parenting standards. Alternatively, it may mean separating the child from the parents, either with their agreement or by means of a court order.

Whilst this system, which is intended to control and regulate parenting, has been in existence since the 1970s, in England and Wales it now operates within the framework of new legislation: the Children Act 1989. This act requires professionals to attempt to work in partnership with parents to find ways to assist them in the task of bringing up their children. It also requires that children's views are sought about what they want and that children should be removed from their parents by order of the courts only as a last resort. The key principle underlying the Children Act is that of working collaboratively with parents. It is not yet clear how the Act will influence social work practice with children at risk. However, the new legislation is in contrast to the more adversarial child protection system, where parents are frequently under suspicion and held to blame for harming their children, and where the possibility of criminal proceedings against parents is never far away.

The Limitations of Current UK Approaches to Children at Risk
Protection or Welfare

Until recently there has been little information available about how the British child protection system was working. However, a number of research studies, funded by the government, have now been completed. Their findings suggest that the system has both strengths and weaknesses. On the plus side, the involvement of a number of agencies in a regulated and ordered system of information exchange and meetings (mainly the police, health and education workers and social workers) means that information from a number of sources is shared, decisions are carefully made and a high proportion of children are protected from further abuse. A number of the recent studies have found that around 70% of the children on child protection registers were not subject to further serious abuse or neglect after entering the child protection system (see for example Farmer and Owen 1995, Gibbons *et al.* 1995). This suggests considerable success at keeping children safe in situations where family members are known to have previously maltreated their children (Barth and Berry 1987, Farmer and Parker, 1991).

On the minus side the studies found that the investigations, during which police officers and social workers question children and their parents, and the large, professionally dominated case conferences which followed, were very stressful for parents who felt shamed and stigmatised and felt that their parenting skills were undermined. This could mean that offers of help from the professionals were refused. Indeed, in some cases parents experienced even *more* difficulty in coping with their children as a result of their involvement in the child protection system. This applied especially where vulnerable mothers were trying to cope with demanding young children or difficult adolescents in impoverished circumstances. The research suggests that these and other parents would have been better served by child care interventions designed to assist them with their difficulties and enhance their parenting skills rather than the monitoring and stigma associated with child protection work (Farmer and Owen 1995, Gibbons *et al* . 1995).

In addition, the research shows that current practice concentrates on immediate protection rather than the child's longer term well-being. It is known that even those children who are removed from home because of abuse are likely to return to live with members of their family once they leave state care (Bullock *et al.* 1993). Yet little emphasis is placed on providing short- or long-term help to the parents on whom these children depend. . . For example, problems, such as an urgent need for rehousing or a parent's mental health difficulties, sometimes receive no assistance from social workers if they are not seen as immediately related to the child's safety. In a similar way a narrow emphasis on child protection can mean that little attention is paid to children's educational and health needs, or to their need for professional help to assist in their recovery from maltreatment (Farmer and Owen 1995).

The Gender of Abusers: Recognising the Source of Risk to Children
All the sexually abused children on the child protection register in the Farmer and Owen study of 44 registered children were abused by men. Physical abuse was inflicted in equal proportions by men and women. In spite of this, the focus of attention, during intervention, was primarily directed at women. In cases of physical abuse by men the attention of professionals moved quickly away from the men and came to rest on the mothers, who were seen as more amenable and available for intervention. This left women in the position of trying to regulate the actions of their partners. This is particularly disturbing because the majority of child deaths in the UK have been caused by men. This shift of focus, from men to women, also allowed men's violence to disappear from sight. The men who physically abused their children were frequently also violent to their wives, yet such domestic violence was rarely accorded much significance in the management of cases. In the Farmer and Owen study most of the children with the worst outcomes were living in families where there was continuing violence by the man to his female partner. This violence was sometimes concealed from the authorities or was considered by professionals as peripheral to their concerns.

In summary, then, the child protection system in the UK pays more attention to controlling families and to identifying children who are at risk than to providing interventions to assist children and their families, such as services designed to rebuild relationships, enhance parenting skills, and help children recover from the experience of abuse. In addition, the risks posed by abusive men are sometimes ignored and insufficient attention has been paid to how to intervene so as to strengthen the support systems of the abused child, which could often be achieved by supporting the non-abusing parent. Not only this, but the child protection system is both intrusive and very expensive to run. It drains resources from other child care services, including the kind of everyday work of supporting and helping needy families which can help to avoid and avert risks to children.

Is More Empowering Practice Possible with Children at Risk?
Empowering social work practice acknowledges the imbalances of power *within families* and in society. It recognises that family members may face disadvantages and discrimination in many aspects of their lives and that these experiences will often have an impact on the health and safety of children. The aim of empowering practice is to reduce and counteract these disadvantages by working with adults and children in a way that helps them ensure that their needs are met and that their rights, feelings and views are appropriately considered by professionals and all other people with whom they have contact.

This concept of 'empowerment' is often thought to be in conflict with the need to protect children from 'dangerous' parents. Clearly, some parents do inflict serious harm or injury to their children and society has a responsibility to try to keep their children safe. Account also needs to be taken of the fact that all young children are physically and emotionally vulnerable and depend on adults for their survival and development. However, we should argue that children's dependency and the fact that the actions of some parents do need regulation do not exclude the possibility of working in an empowering way with parents and children where children are at risk. Empowering practice can be achieved by paying careful attention to which family member or members present risks to a child, by considering the ways in which this risk is increased or diminished by other circumstances in the child's life, and then by developing professional interventions that take account of these factors. In other words, risk assessment and social work interventions, rather than concentrating on the specific details of an abusive event, need to take account of the broader 'protective environment' of the child. This can be defined as 'the range of structural, cultural, personal and interpersonal factors which combine to make the child's world *a more or less safe and fulfilling place'* (Boushel 1994, p.174).

A recent analysis of the cross-national issues relevant to assessing a child's protective environment and to providing support in an empowering way indicates that four elements need to be considered (Boushel 1994). These four elements are, first, power imbalances within families; second, children's needs and rights; third, the support of the wider community, and, finally, the protective safety nets available. Together they form a framework for empowerment in situations where children are at risk. We shall now consider each element in turn.

Recognising Power Imbalances within Families
Gender of abusers
The research findings of Farmer and Owen on the gender of abusers is borne out by many other British and international studies (Creighton 1988, Finkelhor 1986). Within all the societies studied, men were found to be far more likely than women to be the perpetrators of sexual abuse (Finkelhor *et al.* 1986). Typically, these men will have spent considerable time undermining the mother: child relationship and the child's ability to ask for help, so that children will not disclose the abuse or will not be believed if they do so. When account is taken of the amount of time men and women spend with children, British studies indicate that men are also more likely to physically abuse children, although women may be more likely to neglect them (Creighton 1992). When this research is linked with research about the extent of violence to women by husbands or partners (Dobash and Dobash,

1980) it is clear that in many abusive families men may dominate their partners and children by the threat of violence or by undermining women's authority and skill as parents. Until very recently there has been a real professional reluctance to explore the implications of this imbalance of power.

Mothers as Carers

In European societies, as in many others, the work of caring for children is mainly undertaken by women (Condy 1994a and 1994b). Like other aspects of 'women's work' inside and outside the home, this work may not be highly valued, socially or financially, within a society.

The power dynamics within the home may reflect this inequality. Women may have most of the caring responsibility for children and other family members but little of the resources necessary to carry out this responsibility effectively. For example, the adult with the higher income has potentially more control over the family's financial resources and more power in deciding how those resources are used. In most societies, this person is likely to be a man.

In societies where women are taking prime responsibility for childcare, they are also likely to be the major focus of state intervention. By focusing exclusively on women, whether or not they are the adult who has been abusive, and assigning them the main responsibility for the protection of children, social workers all too easily reinforce structural power imbalances.

An approach that takes account of structural disadvantage makes it easier to understand the practical and emotional difficulties that may be faced by women who wish to protect their children from abuse within the family. To translate this into empowering practice social workers need to make sure that they provide a safe opportunity for women to talk about family relationships and how responsibility for childcare and family finances are managed, as well as to discuss any professional concerns about risk to a child. It is equally important that social workers discuss all of these issues directly with the male parent or step-parent and seek to involve him in any plans to protect children. This will mean that the woman is not left with the responsibility for raising professional concerns with her partner and seeking to engage his support.

By exploring the strategies they are *already using* to try and protect their children, it may be possible to work with a mother or non-abusing carer to help strengthen and support those strategies (Boushel and Lebacq 1992). For example, as a short-term measure, a mother may be trying to make sure that her children leave the house to visit a relative at times when their father is most likely to be drunk and violent. Social workers may be able to support this strategy by helping with transport costs, providing food or arranging back-up help when relatives are unavailable. In addition, a woman who is considering fleeing with her children from a violent or sexually abusive man needs somewhere to go that is a safe and adequate alternative. When assessing the protective options open to such parents, it is important to consider the extent to which they are afforded access to supportive financial, legal and other resources by the State, by their community and by their families (Boushel 1994).

Recognising Children's Needs and Rights
How Children Are Valued
To help empower key family members where children are at risk, social workers need to find out from children and other family members who cares about each child and who presents risks to them and why. However, certain categories of children tend to be undervalued in many communities, leaving them potentially vulnerable. These include children with disabilities, children from minority ethnic groups, unhealthy and unwanted children and children born under difficult or stigmatising circumstances (Korbin 1991).

Several issues need consideration in assessing children's experiences. Children may not be equally valued by both of their parents, and some step-parents find it more difficult to value children who are not their own. Other adults in a child's life may either increase risk or help to compensate for problems at home. For example, the child's grandparents or other relatives may be a rich source of affection and protection for children or may contribute to their difficulties. There may be risks too of sexual or physical abuse by older siblings in a family (NCH 1992, Farmer and Owen 1995).

It also needs to be remembered that even when children are highly valued within their families they may be part of a cultural or other sub-group which is not valued by the community and society in which they live. This may lead to harassment, threats and even physical attacks on children outside the home. In creating an extra burden of responsibility for parents this in turn may reinforce any negative attitudes they have towards the child concerned.

Children's Views
Children's perspectives on these issues may be different from those of their parents. They may have both a different view of the problem and see different options for their protection. For example, research suggests that children find it very difficult to tell anyone that they are being sexually abused (Finkelhor *et al.* 1986). As a result, non-abusing parents may have little idea of the extent or nature of the risks. Children who do disclose sexual abuse have varied views about whether they wish

the abuser to be punished and how their own safety can be achieved without damaging relationships with other family members (Farmer and Owen 1995). Where children are at risk outside the home, parents often do not know what is happening or how serious it is, whether this risk is from bullying, alcohol or drug abuse, or other causes (Tizard and Phoenix 1993).

The UN Convention on the Rights of the Child demands that children's views are considered 'in all matters affecting' them (Article 12). Older children may have particular views about their rights and responsibilities which are not shared by their parents. Professional interventions that take account of these views not only empower children but ensure that the plans developed to protect them have a greater chance of success since they can build on the strengths and positive alliances inside and outside the family which children themselves identify.

The Support of the Wider Community
'It takes a whole village to rear a child' (African saying).

Social isolation is often a feature of families where children are abused. This is because risk to children is limited when families are part of a strong social network. Social supports and networks operate in 'the place in between' the family and the support provided by the State. They may allow parents to share child-rearing tasks with others, offer assistance in times of need and provide advice and guidance about parenting. Children's own social networks may provide them with confidantes and role models, with opportunities to feel valued and with models of coping with inappropriate adult behaviour. Social networks also encourage greater consensus about and closer monitoring of acceptable child-rearing practices (Korbin 1991).

In some cases the social isolation experienced by a particular family may be the result of mental illness or be one of the ways in which an abuser tries to ensure that he or she can disempower family members. However, in many other situations it may be that social isolation develops for other reasons, such as lack of time or resources, family migration or social upheaval, cultural attitudes which encourage family privacy, or discrimination within a community towards certain families or groups. Also, within a family some members may be more isolated than others. Social workers need to explore the social networks of different family members in ways that allow these issues to be openly acknowledged. This can help family members consider how to strengthen their social supports in a way that they find acceptable and realistic. It may also be that social workers can encourage the development of new initiatives within a neighbourhood or community so that those adults or children whose social isolation presents a risk have the opportunities necessary to meet other people.

The Availability of Safety Nets

Informal safety nets

The fourth area to consider in developing empowering practice is the availability of adequate support to children who are at immediate risk within their families. Social workers need to consider what formal and informal 'safety nets' exist for individual children and how they might be strengthened. Initially, in a situation of immediate risk, people often turn for help to their informal networks of friends, neighbours and family. Social workers can assist children and their carers to identify exactly who they can turn to, and in what circumstances, when they need help. For example, children may feel able to talk to a trusted teacher or grandparent at times of stress. Communities can also be encouraged to find ways to identify and take care of their most vulnerable members.

Formal Safety Nets

However, there will be situations in which the protection of the State is sought. In a fascinating study which examined 100 years of case records of a child protection agency in Boston, USA, Linda Gordon found that women - mothers, grandmothers and neighbours - often actively sought state help to try and redress abuses of power within the family (Gordon 1989). This was done when other strategies failed. Gordon's research reinforces the importance of taking serious account of such requests for help and of respecting and building on the strategies that parents and others have already developed.

When considering whether to request social work help to protect a child at risk, the quality, availability and acceptability of the 'safety net' services on offer will be an important factor for most parents and children. People will be reluctant to involve state or professional agencies where they suspect that the response of these agencies will be disempowering and may be more harmful than helpful. For example, many state agencies in Britain have a reputation for discriminating against Black people and research has shown that this has meant that Black women are reluctant to seek state help to protect themselves from male violence because they believe that the resources available will neither meet their needs nor treat their male partners in an appropriate way (Mama 1989). Empowering practice by social workers includes an ability to acknowledge the quality of the available professional protective resources and to share that knowledge with family members so that they too can be encouraged to make an informed choice about how best to achieve protection for a child.

Consideration of these four elements indicates that to form a realistic view of the strengths of families, social workers need to be aware of the factors which are most likely to *diminish* risk, as well as those which may increase it. They also need to be aware of the choices and limitations faced by parents as they try to protect their children. Such an understanding helps workers to identify areas in which they can empower children and those who care for them. British research shows that, in spite of the common constraints under which they work, some social workers have been more able to achieve this than others and that parents appreciate workers who approach them in a friendly, respectful and direct way and try to involve them as fully as possible in decisions about their children (Cleaver and Freeman 1995; Farmer and Owen 1995; Thoburn *et al.*1995). These workers were better able to build on the strengths within families and so *work* with family members rather than in *conflict* with them.

Conclusion

From this discussion of current UK research and practice several themes emerge which can help to provide the foundation for empowering practice in situations where children are at risk. They include the need to consider the total context in which *protection* may be provided rather than just concentrating on specific *incidents of abuse*. The professional aim should be to identify and *build on the strengths* of children, their families and their communities, but social workers also need to be clear about *which* family members present risks to the child.

It is important to consider the well-being of children in the *longer term*, rather than simply at the moment of abuse or intervention. This requires attention to both the treatment needs of children and to assisting parents in the task of looking after their children, whether through providing access to services such as day care or through specific forms of help and support. Helping children develop a sense of self-protection is also important for their short- and longer-term safety.

Work with children at risk needs to be approached in both a *child-centred and a parent-centred* way. Practice which is only one or the other is not only potentially dangerous but also fails to address the realities of children's lives. Professionals need to be aware of the *views of children and their parents* about what is harmful for the particular children with whom they work. They need to develop plans which try to find the common ground among professionals, children, and key family members so that they can work together towards common goals.

We cannot avoid the dilemmas involved in our professional responsibility to try and protect children from abuse. But empowering practice can be developed if the views of all those involved are sought and respected, if the choices and limitations they face are acknowledged, and if interventions are developed in a spirit of partnership between professionals and family members.

References

Baldwin, B. and Spencer, N. (1993) 'Deprivation and Child Abuse: Implications for Strategic Planning in Children's Services', *Children and Society,* Vol. 7 No. 4.

Barth, R. P. and Berry, M. (1987) 'Outcomes of child welfare services since permanency planning', *Social Services Review*, Vol. 61, pp.71-90.

Behlmer, G. (1982) *Child Abuse and Moral Reform in England 1870-1908,* Stanford, CA, Stanford University Press.

Boushel, M. and Lebacq, M. (1992) 'Towards Empowerment in Child Protection Work', *Children & Society*, Vol.6, pp.38-50.

Boushel, M. (1994) 'The Protective Environment of Children: Towards a Framework for Anti-Oppressive, Cross-Cultural and Cross-National Understanding', *British Journal of Social Work*, 24: 173-90.

Bullock, R.; Little, M, and Milham, S. (1993) *Going Home*, Dartmouth.

Cleaver, H. and Freeman, P. (1995) *Parental Perspectives in Cases of Suspected Child Abuse*, London, HMSO.

Coffield, F., Borrill, C., and Marshall, S. (1986) *Growing up at the Margins*, Milton Keynes, Open University Press.

Condy, A. (1994a) 'Families and Caring', *Factsheet 4*, International Year of the Family 1994, Family Policies Study Centre, London.

Condy, A. (1994b) 'Parents and Families', *Factsheet 5*, International Year of the Family 1994, Family Policies Study Centre, London.

Creighton, S. (1992) *Child Abuse Trends in England and Wales*, London, NSPCC.

Department of Health (1991) *Child Abuse. A Study of Inquiry Reports 1980-1989*, London, HMSO.

Department of Health and Social Security (1976) *Non-Accidental Injury to Children*, LASSI (76)2.

Department of Health and Social Security (1980) *Child Abuse: Central Register Systems*, LASSL (80)4: HN (80)20.

Department of Health and Social Security (1982) *Child Abuse: A Study of Inquiry Reports 1973-1981*, London, HMSO.

Dingwall, R., Eekelaar, J., and Murray, T. (1983) *The Protection of Children: State Intervention and Family Life*, Oxford, Blackwell.

Dobash, R. E. and Dobash, R. (1980) *Violence Against Wives,* Basingstoke, Macmillan.

Farmer, E. and Owen, M. (1995) *Child Protection Practice: Private Risks and Public Remedies*, London, HMSO.

Farmer, E. and Parker, R. (1991) *Trials and Tribulations: Returning Children from Local Authority Care to their Families,* London, HMSO.

Finkelhor, D. (1991) 'The Lazy Revolutionary's Guide to the Prospects of Reforming Child Welfare', *Child Abuse and Neglect* 15, Suppl. 17-23

Finkelhor, D.; Araji, S.; Baron, L.; Browne, A.; Doyle Peters, S. and Wyatt, G. E. (1986) *A Sourcebook on Child Sexual Abuse,* Beverley Hills, California: Sage.

Gibbons, J.; Conroy, S.; and Bell, C. (1995) *Operation of Child Protection Registers,* London, HMSO.

Gordon, L. (1989) *Heroes of Their Own Lives,* London, Virago Press.

Kempe, C. H.; Silverman, F. N.; Steele, B. F.; Droegmueller, W. and Silver, H. K. (1962) 'The battered child syndrome', *Journal of the American Medical Association,* No. 181, pp.17-22.

Korbin, J. (1991) 'Cross-Cultural Perspectives and Research Directions for the 21st Century', *Child Abuse and Neglect* 15, Suppl.1: pp.67-77.

Kumar, V. (1993) *Poverty and Inequality in the UK: The Effects on Children,* London, National Children's Bureau.

London Borough of Brent (1985) *A Child in Trust.* The Report of the Panel of Inquiry into the Circumstances Surrounding the Death of Jasmine Beckford.

Mama, A. (1989) *The Hidden Struggle,* Runnymede Trust: London Race and Housing Research Unit.

National Children's Home (1992) *The Report of the Committee of Enquiry into Children and Young People Who Sexually Abuse Other Children,* London, NCH.

Parker, R. (1995) 'A Brief History of Child Protection' in Farmer, E., and Owen, M. Child Protection Practice: *Private Risks and Public Remedies,* London, HMSO.

Parton, N. (1985) *The Politics of Child Abuse,* Basingstoke, Macmillan.

Secretary of State for Social Services (1988), *Report of the Inquiry into Child Abuse in Cleveland 1987,* Cm 412, London, HMSO.

Thoburn J.; Lewis, A. and Shemmings, D. (1995) *Paternalism or Partnership? Family Involvement in the Child Protection Process,* London, HMSO.

Tizard, B. and Phoenix, A. (1993) *Black, White and Mixed Race: Race and Racism in the Lives of Young People of Mixed Parentage,* 1st ed., London: Routledge.

Van Montfoort, A. (1993) 'The Protection of Children in the Netherlands: Between Justice and Welfare' in *Surviving Childhood Adversity,* Dublin: Social Studies Press, Trinity College

European Views

British systems for co-ordinating a multi-professional response to risk of abuse are generally highly regarded by Continental colleagues. However, the very limited provision for day care and other preventive services for young children and their families, and what is often regarded as an intrusive and punitive approach to families in difficulties, have been the subject of criticism. Other European countries have dealt with the dilemma of state intervention in family life by different means. In several, the main emphasis is on prevention of risk through universal health and day-care services for young children and some support for parents, especially mothers. In cases of serious risk, there are diverse approaches (Sale and Davies 1990, Spencer *et al.* 1989). In France the judicial system takes over responsibility and social workers act on the instruction of the judge. In Holland, on the other hand, a family may be referred to a medically based therapeutic service in which social workers are part of the therapeutic team. At present, because of varying methods of data collection, it is not possible to compare the outcomes of the different approaches.

Sale, A. and Davies, M. (eds) (1990) *Child Protection Policies and Practice in Europe*, London: NSPCC, Occasional Paper no. 9.

Spencer, J. R.; Nicholson, G.; Flin, R. and Bull, R. (1989) *Children's Evidence in Legal Proceedings: An International Perspective*, Cambridge, Spencer.

Part III
Ways of working
towards empowerment

Helping Individuals to Take Power

Phyllida Parsloe

Summary

This chapter considers the conditions which a social worker can attempt to create which may allow clients to take more power over their own lives - to empower themselves. These conditions include a relationship between worker and client, the need for the worker to attempt to understand the client's personal meanings and to be aware of his or her own prejudices; and the thoughtful use of language. How worker and client can share the choice of methods of work including recording is also addressed.

Despite the recent frequent use of the word "empowerment", most social workers would probably agree that it is not possible for one person to empower another; in fact the very suggestion that this could be the case is disempowering. What is possible is to create conditions in which it may be possible for clients themselves to take power over their own lives - to empower themselves.

What then are those conditions? They consist in:

A positive relationship between client and social worker.

A determination on the part of the social worker to understand the client.

Self-awareness and skill in the social worker.

Careful use of language.

A shared way of working.

A shared use of records.

A relationship

There have been many attempts to define social work in the United States and in Britain but none have been taken up by social workers as providing a clear brief statement of the core of their activity. I personally find Bill Jordan's statement helpful. He suggests that social work consists of delivering social services in a social work way. Obviously that risks being tautological unless one goes on to spell out in which a "social work way" consists. Clearly it has to be different from other ways of delivering services such as a family way, a bureaucratic way or a commercial way. How it differs, I would suggest, is that a social work way of delivering services presupposes that a relationship exists between client and social worker and the purpose of that relationship, from the social worker's point of

111

view, is to ensure that the views and needs of the client are taken into account in the delivery of services. The relationship means that the social worker becomes accountable to the client as well as to his or her profession and agency.

In the 1950s and 1960s there was much written about the nature of this social work relationship. Then the idea seemed to go underground for a while. Of course social workers went on developing relationships with the people they worked with but it was less fashionable to talk or write about this relationship. Social work methods and social work skills were more likely to be the subject of articles and of teaching and the personal and moral nature of social work was hidden. In Britain, more recently there is a revival of interest in the importance of a relationship, especially before adequate assessments of need can be carried out. Social workers, who are employed as care managers and whose task is to assess, with elderly and disabled people, their care needs, are explaining to their managers that it is not possible to carry out a "needs-led assessment" until one has a relationship with the user.

The term "needs-led" has been adopted in Britain to describe an assessment which focuses not upon fitting people into available services – a service-led approach – but upon understanding individual needs and then finding services to meet them. But this is not a simple process as Olive Stevenson and I (1993) explained when discussing the notion of need within the context of community care.

"The notion of need is extremely wide. It ranges from 'I need something to enable me to move around the house' to 'I need something to do': from 'I need to find a flat' to 'I need a partner to share my life with'. When the 'need' goes to the roots of a person's being, it requires a shift from describing a feeling state – 'I feel low in myself' – to an articulation of what is missing – 'I need more company'.

"This is difficult for some people. Indeed, even putting into words what they feel may be hard for many, not least if they are cognitively, physically or sensorially impaired, or when mental distress clouds their capacity to clarify feelings and to express themselves. The first tasks of the worker, therefore, may be to help put feelings into words and the deeper the feelings, the harder they may be to capture, as in the case of many old people who feel their lives lack purpose."

Putting feelings into words is difficult for many people and the more painful the feelings, the harder it is. An intimate stranger, as a social worker can be, may be the person to whom it is easiest to speak, especially when he or she is skilled at naming these often unspoken feelings and thus allowing them to be brought into conscious awareness. This process requires skill in the worker and trust by the client and is the more likely to happen when the client feels the worker is relating to him or her as a person.

The same is true for the next step in the assessment, which is the translation of feelings into needs. As Stevenson and I explain:

"Once a feeling has been articulated and shaped into need, there is still another stage. The user or carer may say 'I am lonely and have nowhere to go'. He or she may not know there is a drop-in centre or may not feel comfortable in that environment. Some users may appear unrealistic in what they want. We heard of one man who was mentally ill who did not want to go to the day centre but said he wanted to go to art galleries in Amsterdam. In fact, that proved feasible and released a wealth of knowledge and enthusiasm, hitherto hidden from the worker, about art.

"At other times, the expressed need may be totally unrealistic but it reveals interests which can be built upon, as in the case of which we were told, of the man who wanted to be a croupier. In moving towards that goal (which he was told he was unlikely to achieve), he learnt maths and other relevant skills. The task of the worker therefore, is to turn the expressed need into a concrete plan which is feasible."

These apparently simple steps are essential if the aim is to create a situation in which the client can feel, to the greatest possible extent, in charge of his or her own life and of the decisions which have to be made about services.

Understanding

If clients are to find confidence and power, social workers will also need to understand the range of complex feelings which underlie seeking help or being assessed for services. A few can be mentioned here. Some people may feel they are unworthy and such feelings are not confined to those who are clinically depressed. Many of us, perhaps particularly if we are women, feel we are not worth other people's concern and feel guilty at asking for help. With such clients, the task of the worker is to accept those feelings and attempt to raise self-esteem, in part through the relationship. The worker seeks to move the user or carer on to consideration of their entitlement to support, a crucial element in notions of empowerment.

Others may be too embarrassed to say what they need, especially if it concerns sexual relationships or the control of bodily functions. Yet others may not want to talk and may have little reason, based on experience, to trust officials. With such clients the first task for the worker is to begin to build a relationship which can open the way to communication and then to the client having increased power over their lives.

The kind of understanding which may lead to clients feeling empowered requires what Baldock and Ungerson (1994), borrowing from de Tocquiville, call a knowledge of "the habits of the heart". He described these as "notions, opinions and ideas that shape mental habits; the sum of moral and intellectual dispositions of people in society; not only ideas and opinions but habitual practices with respect to such things as religion, political participation and economic life".

Baldock and Ungerson develop this idea in an attempt to explain why some people, recovering from a stroke, found it difficult to adjust to their new, and often more restricted, lives and accept services from others. They suggest that when people need social care services, their previous life experience will determine the way in which they involve themselves in seeking and accepting services. People carry with them unacknowledged expectations which propel them towards high and low participation in the management of their own affairs and also a tendency towards an individualistic or collectivist approach. On this basis the authors suggest four model types of participation in the care market:

"Habits of the heart": models of participation in the care market

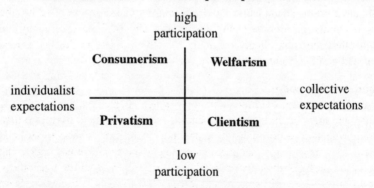

Baldock and Ungerson define these model types as follows:-

Consumerism - a view that expects nothing from the State and tends to arrange care by actively buying it in the market or providing it out of household or family resources.

Privatism - attention is devoted to home- and family-based life . . . a rather passive form of consumerism where most of the work is done by producers and retailers and requires little initiative from consumers other than the act of purchase itself.

Welfarism - a belief in the Welfare State and the right to use it - the active pursuit of one's entitlements.

Clientism - the traditional way of using the Welfare State - passive, accepting, patient and grateful.

The model types which Baldock and Ungerson have developed may not fit all, or indeed any, cultures. However, the idea of "habits of the heart" is one that can be adapted to any race, culture or political system and it provides a useful tool for social workers intent upon helping clients to change. Any change in behaviour requires an alteration to underlying habits and assumptions and these must be taken into account when assisting clients to take control of aspects of their lives and therefore to change.

This discussion provides only one example of a way in which social workers need to attempt to understand their clients if clients are to feel empowered. Attempts to understand may be made more difficult when the client and the social worker are of different genders, widely separated in age or of different races. Such differences should alert the social worker to the possibility that they will not grasp the meaning of events and proposed solutions for their clients. If necessary they can check what they see as the client's meaning with others whose gender, age or race is closer to that of the client.

Skills and self-awareness
Creating relationships, providing a climate in which clients feel able to talk and then understanding something of the meaning of other people's lives is skilled work, requiring a capacity to listen to feelings as well as words, to suspend judgement, to manage one's own feelings, and yet to be spontaneous, honest and real. Some people by birth or upbringing have more of these qualities than others. Almost all can if they wish, and should, if they want to work with people, learn these skills.

Skills alone are not enough to help other people to gain self-esteem, confidence and power. Social workers also require sufficient self-awareness to recognise their own prejudices and assumptions in order to protect their clients from the negative effects these can have. Since social workers have grown up in societies where there are common prejudices, they will share them. Like their fellow citizens they are likely to see certain categories of people as in some ways less worthy than others. Racism (towards, for example, black people and gypsies), sexism and ageism are part of the cultural air we breathe in Britain. Before social workers can hope to help those who are oppressed by such prejudices, they must recognise their own culturally acquired tendencies.

Such cultural prejudices are now widely acknowledged in social work in Britain. What is less obvious but equally important is the tendency in many of us, social workers included, to behave as if we know what is best for other people. Such attitudes are inimical to empowering practice and yet are widespread. Marsh and Fisher (1992), in their account of some action research in which care managers aimed to work in partnership with clients, found that all too often the social workers' good intentions were thwarted by their habitual response. This was to fail to hear what users wanted and to take over from them. The notion of giving help seems to be inextricably associated with telling people what they should do and with doing things for them, processes which are experienced by the recipient as disempowering and which perhaps explain why many people feel ashamed at the thought that they need help. Social workers have to unlearn this approach to helping and put in its place an approach which enables clients to decide what they want for themselves.

Language

The tool of social work is language: language of the voice and language of the body. Social workers in Britain are often accused of using jargon. This is undoubtedly true at times and is quite unnecessary since what social workers deal with is the everyday events and feelings of people's lives which need no jargon to understand or to describe. Often the language used is not exactly jargon in the sense of a technical language of the subject, but rather the use of long and somewhat pretentious words when there are everyday, usually shorter, alternatives. Examples of this tendency drawn from reports written by probation officers are:

- The woman almost always "presents as . . ."
- The court appearance often had a "salutary" effect
- Some women "prematurely depart treatment"
- Some admit "proximity to the disturbance"

116

–   Some aim "to change in a positive manner"
–   They are "remorseful" about their "offending behaviour"
       (Parsloe 1995).

Some research by Horsley (1984) analysed the reading age required to understand some probation reports and then tested the reading age of the person who was the subject of the report. In all the cases she investigated there was a gap of several years between the two which would mean that the subject would not be able to understand the report about her and was therefore in no position to question its contents.

In selecting what to say or write and how to say it, social workers may find it helpful to listen very carefully to the language used by their clients and, in some ways, to follow it. Bandler and Grindler (1976), in a fascinating book called *The Structure of Magic*, suggest that people differ in the way they understand the world; some seem to "see" it, others to "hear", and yet others, although these are rare, to "touch" it. The notions of seeing and hearing are built into our language and almost any piece of conversation is likely to contain such phrases as "do you *see* what I mean?", or "yes, I *hear* what you say". These authors suggest that communication is helped when both people adopt an approach employing the same sensibilities. I have found that this idea has made me very attentive to other people's speech patterns and aware of my overwhelming tendency to use and impose on others a visual approach.

Bandler and Grindler go on to suggest that similar attention to our own and our client's body movements can aid communication. They suggest that it is possible to help clients alter their mood by the use of one's own body language. Sometimes a very tense client who is sitting forward with clenched hands can be helped to relax not only by words used and tone of voice employed but also by the worker consciously adopting and holding a relaxed posture. We tend to copy each other's bodily stance, and awareness of this can increase our range of language.

I am not, of course, suggesting that social workers should adopt all their client's spoken or bodily conventions. For example, for a middle-aged social worker to adopt the language of a teenage client would be likely to be experienced by the client as either ridiculous or patronising. Nevertheless, attention to language can help to create a feeling of equality between worker and client.

Of course, the actual content matters greatly. Attention to form is no substitute for careful choice in what is actually said. It is often the most obvious things that are omitted. I spend a good deal of time watching video recordings of student social workers interviewing either real or role-playing clients. What strikes me is how often they fail to say who they are and to make sure the client actually hears their names: to state why they have come and, at the end of a meeting, to summarise the next steps. A recent piece of research (Baldwin and Ungerson 1994) found that many people from a group of clients who had had a full assessment undertaken by a social worker for the local social services department did not even know they had been assessed. When they remembered someone calling, they seldom knew where he or she came from or why, and even less often did they know the name of the person or how to get hold of them again. The tendency amongst professional staff to use their first names, presumably to indicate a friendly approach, was unhelpful in establishing their identity. These meetings must have been mystifying for the clients and to have contributed little to their sense of control over their own lives.

Honest explanations, even of unpleasant facts, are what clients are looking for. This has been demonstrated over and over again in the literature on users' views of social work. What users appreciate and what they find helps their self-confidence are workers who are honest and straightforward, not afraid of being themselves, and who make clear the reality of the situation which the client faces.

Choice of ways of working
So far I have written largely as if the contact between client and worker is short term and for the purpose of undertaking a needs-led assessment. However, much social work involves a longer period of contact and has as its aim helping a client to alter some aspect of their behaviour or circumstances. Such longer-term work can involve choices about who is to be involved in the work and the methods to be used.

Who to involve may raise difficult ethical issues as the following case illustrates (Stevenson and Parsloe 1993). It is the story of "Maria" as told by the worker. Maria is 16. At the point at which the worker came on the scene, Maria had been allowed to stay at home without schooling for over 10 years. Offers from the education department over the years had all been rejected by her mother and Maria remained "cocooned" at home. As the worker wrote:

> She has not experienced much of the outside world and has been prevented
> from making peer group contact. The training and specialist teaching which
> might have allowed her to learn speech or other forms of communication
> have been denied her. Her behaviour is difficult and disruptive. She is
> doubly incontinent. Her mother says she is unable to feed herself and only
> eats minced foods. Maria in short is totally dependent on her mother and
> her mother, in turn, believes it is her duty and role in life to look after a child
> such as Maria.

Dilemma

Does Maria have a right to experience those things which most of us take for granted?

Does she have the right to the basic dignity of being independent in her personal care: of toileting herself, of feeding herself, and enjoying different textures and tastes?

Should she be given the opportunity to learn to communicate with other people? Should she be taught to, and be expected to, behave appropriately?

If all this cannot be done with her mother's co-operation, should it still be attempted?

In short, who has the right and who should have the responsibility to decide on the quality of life for Maria?

Plan

To make as quickly as possible a thorough assessment of Maria's abilities, potential and her needs.

To start to build a relationship with her mother. To try to understand why she is unwilling to allow other professionals and agencies to be involved in the support and training of Maria. To persuade her to work with us and to let Maria experience other things away from home.

To get to know Maria in order to start to consider the benefits of her present situation. To assess whether Maria is at risk where she is.

To ascertain what facilities and training could be suitable for and be offered to Maria within and outside the home.

To arrange for her future to be discussed in a multi-disciplinary setting with shared responsibility for that future by all those involved.

To arrange within six months to be in a position to make a long-term plan for Maria as a young adult.

Action

To date, the early work is going well.

Maria, her mother and grandmother have accepted that I will be visiting more regularly. The visits have been friendly and productive.

Mother and I have to a limited extent looked at why I would be wishing to plan for Maria's future. She has tacitly acknowledged that I am concerned and could look to the new Children Act for backing those concerns if she is not co-operative.

119

*My own initial assessment has been followed up by a joint assessment with
the manager from the Local Support Unit for Adults with Learning
Disabilities. A Clinical Psychologist will shortly be making a more specific
assessment of Maria's abilities.*

*Meantime I am conscious I must focus on Maria as my client. I have to not
only look at what might be available to her and how she would gain from
that, but also address the losses that might have to be accepted in order for
her to achieve more from home.*

*When I look at her interacting with and being totally dependent on her
mother, it is difficult not to collude with them and allow the status quo to
continue unchallenged. Will she thank us for changing things now? Can
she take advantage of the environment outside her home now? Will she be
better off - or is it too late?*

This case illustrates the ethical issues in the exercise of social power. The
principle of empowerment is central to the work but is qualified by the limitations
of all those involved and the pre-existing situation. There is no right answer but
equally there is no neutral position. Working towards empowerment raises
questions of value no less than any other form of social work.

The actual way of working with a client can contribute or detract from the creation
of an empowering situation. It seems appropriate that clients should be offered a
choice of the ways in which they and the social worker will work together. This
means that the social worker must be competent and confident in the use of a
range of methods and able to spell out clearly to a client their particular features.
For example, it should be possible to discuss with clients whether they consider
that their past experiences are important in their present situation and whether
they would like to talk about the past and its relevance for the present or concentrate solely on the present. Clients should also choose between methods that
involve largely reflection or mainly prescribed action and the extent to which they
want to agree on tasks to be undertaken between sessions. In my experience, most
people have a clear preference as to how to work if they are given the chance to
understand the issues and then to choose.

The worker will also have to ensure that the methods he or she offers are not disempowering or, if they have a tendency to be so, that steps are taken to alter or
omit particular aspects. Task-focused work is a case in point. It is sometimes
regarded as a method which shares power and responsibility between client and
worker since the pair agree on tasks to be undertaken, in what time span and by
which of the pair. What determines whether it increases the client's power is the

extent to which the worker enables the client to have a real choice about what is done and who does it. This is to shift the traditional approach in which the worker at least tacitly controls the process and allocates the tasks to one where the client has equal power and can therefore decide what the worker will do.

Other methods of work can have equally disempowering features; for example, some forms of counselling in which interpretations of past events are made by the worker. An alternative to interpretations is a joint search for explanations.

The idea of explaining the process is another way of increasing the client's control over the interactions. I notice that my social work students find this difficult to do, perhaps because they are not yet confident in handling process as well as content. However, it is often helpful to explain. For example, I was recently working with a young woman who had panic attacks. She had decided they were connected to her childhood and wanted to discuss the past but had great difficulty remembering anything about it. As she talked I noticed she seemed to be shrinking into a corner of the chair and I mentioned this and said I was doing so because I did not understand it since I was not threatening her. I told her it reminded me of a child in a corner she could not get out of. I went on to say that this might just reflect my childhood rather than hers but I did believe that sometimes our bodies acted out the past when our minds could not put these experiences into words. It would be nice to say she was immediately able to talk about her past but that was not the case. That came later and after a lot more explanation on my part.

In summarising, what I am suggesting here is that when the intention is to empower, then the worker must take all possible steps to share what he or she is doing with the client so that the client does not feel in the grip of a process she or he neither understood nor controlled. The worker must abandon professional mystique for the more difficult but ultimately more satisfying position of an equal relationship.

Not all continuing contacts with clients are of their choosing and the question of empowerment, in situations where the worker is required to control the client, raises difficult issues. Is control essentially disempowering? I do not think it need be although it requires great skill and confidence on the part of the worker and certain personal attributes in the client to ensure it is not. What is essential is that the areas of control are clearly spelt out and understood by the client and that his or her right to choice or to opt out is maintained in all other areas. So, for example, a mother whose child has been abused by her now-separated partner may not be allowed to let the man return to the home without the child being removed into care. But that may be the extent to which the social worker controls the mother's actions, and any other aspects of her life are within her control. She can choose whether or not to share them with the social worker.

Records

The final aspect of an empowering situation which social workers need to consider is the question of the records they keep about clients. Most people feel uneasy, if not actually frightened, at the idea of records being kept about them. In Britain, citizens now have a right to see what is recorded about them in either manual or computerised social work records. This right is limited only by the rights of others to confidentiality and by the likelihood of access causing serious harm to the subject or someone else. These relatively recent laws have led to elaborate procedures in social service agencies by which clients can see their records. Few actually do so and the law is therefore insufficient by itself. In some agencies social workers have developed joint recording with clients so that at the end of a meeting the worker will write with the client the notes of the meeting which will go into the file. A few social workers and some doctors have gone further and ask the client to keep the record.

Clients should ask not only what is in their records but who beside themselves and their worker can see them; to what extent are they confidential? Social workers tend to assure clients that what they say is confidential but without always explaining where the limits of confidentiality lie. This is an area where agency policies are essential so that staff can explain to clients exactly what is and is not meant by confidential records.

Social workers reading this chapter are likely to consider that the ways which have been described as likely to help a client to achieve more power are no more than good social work practice. This is true, but good practice is not easy to achieve in the complex, changing, often painful, human world within which social workers and clients meet each other.

References

Baldock, J. and Ungerson, C. (1994). *Becoming Consumers of Community Care*. Joseph Rowntree Foundation. York

Bandler, R. and Grindler, J. (1976). *The Structure of Magic*. Palo Alto. Science and Behaviour books

Jordan, B. and Parton, N. (1981). *The Political Dimensions of Socialm Work*. Basil Blackwell. Oxford

Marsh, P. and Fisher, M. (1992). *Good intentions*. Joseph Rowntree Foundation. York

Parsloe, P. (1995). *Pre-sentence reports about Women from Bristol*, p.32. Bristol University

Stevenson, O. and Parsloe, P. (1993). *Community Care and Empowerment*. Joseph Rowntree Foundation. York

Groups as a Means of Empowerment:
Facilitating Self-directed Change

Audrey Mullender

This chapter outlines the self-directed approach to groupwork which is seen as a particularly effective way of promoting participation and empowerment through groups. The groupworkers' facilitating role and anti-oppressive value-base are seen as fundamental tenets of the approach. The stages through which self-directed groups move are shown as being organised around a series of key questions; techniques which workers can employ to pose these questions to a group are described and illustrated by practice examples.

A group is a powerful medium for empowerment and for change because it can be greater than the sum of its parts: people can achieve more together than they can separately. Group members can, for example, combine together to find new solutions to old problems either for themselves as individuals or in relation to wider issues which cause difficulties for whole categories of people. It is groups targeted at the second of these aims – that of wider-scale change – with which this chapter will be concerned.

The particular approach which will be proposed here is known as self-directed groupwork (Mullender and Ward, 1985, 1991). It is part of a long tradition in groupwork involving social action and is based on a clear set of practice principles which engage directly with changes external to the group. As part of this effort for change, groupworkers and members work to alter negative attitudes and unequal power dynamics. The underpinning practice principles of self-directed groupwork embody: an anti-oppressive view of those we work with; a belief that they have the ability to define their own problems, set their own goals and take their own action for change; a commitment to basing this change on broader social analysis than is commonly the case, certainly in most professional intervention; and a style of working in partnership with people which facilitates and empowers them to move in the direction they choose.

The self-directed approach is also founded on the belief that people have a right to join together to ask themselves questions about the problems they confront in their lives and to seek their own solutions – even if, as a result, they see the cause of the problems as ultimately social or political. No system of social or political organisation knows or seeks what is best for everyone in a benignly neutral way or should ever be given total control over our lives. Change for the better typically comes from people standing up for what they believe in - be this a cleaner environment, a fairer system of government or justice, or improved health and welfare services, for example. Seeking such change can begin in quite a small way, through groups, and may sometimes spread nationwide. A good example is the women's refuge movement in Britain. This began with one small group of women protesting about the ending of free school milk (Dobash and Dobash, 1992: p.25), progressed through these and then other women meeting together to discuss the circumstances of their lives, and has culminated to date in the existence of over 200 refuges (safe houses) in England and Wales alone, where women and their children can escape men's violence towards them. Although the refuge movement still is not satisfied with this pace or degree of progress, it has achieved major changes in housing and benefits policies which increase the chances of women beginning a new life in safety.

The early women's groups did not have workers but ran along egalitarian, self-run lines. The challenge to social workers and others who work with groups is to assist those who may feel impotent and helpless to improve their lives to emulate the vision and energy of campaigning groups which spring up spontaneously. Traditionally, the role of a social worker has too often meant 'knowing best'; it has stifled rather than encouraged spontaneous action for change. Social work and groupwork can only be empowering if social workers recognise that no one knows more than service users about the problems which confront them, and that a modest injection of encouragement and skilled support - in the context of the shared strength of a group - may make it perfectly possible to begin tackling wider social problems together.

Participation in Self-Directed Groups
Self-directed groupwork involves the maximum participation by group members. Self-direction implies drawing out the strengths in group members and helping them to determine where they want the group to go, as opposed to the groupworkers imposing their own aims or direction. In order to achieve this, groupworkers need to define their overall role not as leaders but as *facilitators* (Ward and Mullender, 1991).

Initially, this can be a frustrating and unfamiliar role. It can also be very time-consuming. Developments would usually be quicker and more predictable if the workers went ahead and took decisions. The refusal to be directive can be difficult both for workers and for members, but the process is none the less necessary if service users are to take responsibility for decisions and events through involvement in groups. It is especially difficult for workers with a background in statutory social work - who may be more used to taking decisions for themselves and others – to sit back and consciously stop themselves from directing the decisions of a group, leaving it to move at its own pace and learn from its own mistakes.

Often, people who are unfamiliar with the facilitator's role but enthusiastic about it fall into the trap of going too far the other way and becoming totally non-intervenient. This is not what is implied by facilitation. The concept involves playing an active role but being sensitive to the differences between this and a dominant one. It means resisting the sense of passive acceptance which members can bring to a group, especially at the beginning. It does not mean falling over backwards to keep oneself and one's own views invisible and unheard.

A clear example of this is that there are some things workers will be prepared to be involved in, and others not. They have the right to say so. Since involvement is constructed as a partnership of workers and users, it would be dishonest for workers not to share the things they feel strongly about. It could also mean that they colluded with the group in being oppressive of others. Workers' expectations and assumptions are easily taken for granted, as being in agreement with the group, if left unspoken. In a group of young offenders, for example, sexist and racist remarks by group members were confronted because they were issues about which the workers had developed their own fundamental practice principles. Oppressive comments were discussed and challenged as and when they occurred. It is essential for facilitators to be honest with members about their 'bottom line', about what they can and cannot accept.

As well as needing to think carefully about their facilitative role for the sake of their own clarity in practice, workers need to work hard at explaining and maintaining this role in the group. Members will be more used to professionals as figures of authority, and as providers or withholders of resources. Consequently, they will expect the workers to tell them what to do and how to do it, and to procure everything the group needs to make it function. It takes frequent direct explanation and practical demonstrations for group members to recognise that they can look to the workers for help but not for instruction. Workers have initially to be directive about being non-directive. They must hold strongly to offering techniques and processes which will best facilitate the group to achieve its aims, but should not attempt to influence what those aims will be. Like all groupworkers, those employing the self-directed approach benefit from the support of an experienced consultant (Mullender and Ward, 1993). He or she can offer particular assistance in helping them clarify their values before starting the group, in bringing them back to their practice principles as the group proceeds, and in holding the balance between moving the group forward on the one hand and not encroaching on setting its goals on the other.

As the group progresses and matures, its members will grow in confidence. Early successes in achieving small-scale change – perhaps in gaining some positive publicity for the group in the media, or persuading a public official to reverse an unpopular decision – will help considerably in bolstering members' belief in what they and the group can accomplish. Over time, group members will move beyond being able to select the overall goals for the group into learning from the group-workers' ways of moving the group forward. There is no mystique about these techniques or about the workers' knowledge of group dynamics. With experience, group members can begin to take responsibility for group process as well as group content, for means as well as ends. Although this may take many months, it is the stage at which the group becomes truly self-directing.

Empowering Principles

Maximising the participation of group members is only one aspect of empowerment. It would not be empowering to be told that you can choose what to do in a group but still to be treated in a condescending or disapproving way. Social work which assumes or emphasises pathology and weakness in service users, rather than strength and potential, is frequently disempowering.

At the heart of the self-directed model of groupwork lies a set of practice principles which are inherently empowering and which can even be used as a test of how empowering a group is likely to be. Far from being written deliberately as a prescriptive recipe for groups to follow, these principles have been drawn from observing and working with a range of groups which have achieved self-direction and empowerment. They constitute the value position on which empowering groupwork is based:

1. Groupworkers need to take a view of the people with whom they work which refuses to accept negative labels and recognises that all people have skills, understanding and ability.

2. People have rights, including the right to be heard and the right to control their lives. It follows that they also have the right to choose what kinds of intervention to accept in their lives. Service users must always be given the right to decide whether or not to participate in self-directed work, and the right to define issues and act on them.

3.   The problems users face are complex and can never be fully understood if they are seen solely as a result of personal inadequacies. Issues of oppression, social policy, the environment and the economy are, more often then not, major contributory forces. Practice should reflect this understanding.

4.   Effective practice can be built on the knowledge that people acting collectively can be powerful. People who lack power can gain it through working together in groups.

5.   All our work must challenge oppression whether by reason of race, gender, sexual orientation, age, class or wealth, disability, or any other form of social differentiation upon which spurious notions of superiority and inferiority are built and kept in place by the abuse of power.

6.   Methods of working must reflect these non-élitist principles. The worker does not 'lead' the group but facilitates decision making and responsibility for and control of outcomes. Though special skills and knowledge are employed in assisting the group, these do not accord privilege and are not the sole province of the worker.

Stages of the Model: Asking the Key Questions
These practice principles, together with the facilitative worker role, add up to a distinctive approach. They allow the groupworkers, who typically work in combinations of two or three, to help the group move through a number of stages in the direction of the external change members want to achieve. These stages are organised into a number of steps which, following on from the worker team's establishment of its own value position, are based on assisting the group to ask itself certain key questions. The stages are as follows.

Stage One: Taking Stock
(a)   The workers begin by formulating a coherent value position along the lines of the practice principles outlined earlier. They accept empowerment of service users as a valid aim to be pursued by addressing structural issues in day-to-day practice. The workers consider potential group members to have strengths, skills and understanding. They see them as having the ability to do things for themselves through the group and something to offer one another.

(b)   Once the workers have reached agreement on these matters, they can invite people who share a particular structural problem to choose to join the group. Group members become partners with the worker team in seeking solutions to wider social issues.

Stage Two: Taking Action
The group moves from recognition to action as it is helped to explore the questions

'WHAT?', 'WHY?' AND 'HOW?'.

(c)   The workers facilitate the group in setting its own agenda of issues: *ASKING THE QUESTION - 'WHAT?'*

(d)   The workers help the group to analyse why the problems on its agenda exist: *ASKING THE QUESTION - 'WHY?'*

(e)   The workers enable members to decide what actions to take. (Workers do not impose their own ideas for action, except to say they will not do certain things such as working towards racist goals.) The group's members share the tasks. *ASKING THE QUESTION – 'HOW?'*

(f)   The members take those actions for themselves.

Stages (c) to (f) may recur several times during the 'Taking Action' stage.

Stage Three: Taking Over
The group is helped to perceive the connections between *'WHAT?', 'WHY?' and 'HOW?'*

(g)   The group reviews what it has achieved.

(h)   The group identifies new issues to be tackled: *REFORMULATING 'WHAT?'*

(i)   The group perceives the links between the different issues tackled: *REFORMULATING 'WHY?'*

(j)   The group decides what actions to take next: *REFORMULATING 'HOW?'*

Steps (g) to (j) become a recurring process for the life of the group.

Group members gradually gain some control over their own lives and realise that they have a right to more. They are now active in tackling the roots of their own oppression. In Stage Three, the workers have moved into the background.

Techniques for Posing the Key Questions
The work of posing each question in the group may take many weeks or months. At all times, the workers are active in maximising participation, stimulating motivation and encouraging and supporting members to express and tackle their problems through the group. The workers achieve much of this work through the use of particular techniques which throw the responsibility for making decisions and setting priorities back to group members. Some examples of these techniques, with accounts of groups using them, will now be offered.

Asking the Question 'WHAT?'
The first area of activity, once an initial working agreement has been reached between workers and participants (Mullender and Ward, 1989), is for the group to begin its search for collectively agreed goals. The groupworkers' first priority is to find ways of helping service users to express all the concerns which are at the forefront of their lives so that they can go on to determine their own agenda of issues. This is summed up by asking the question 'WHAT?'

One of the classic techniques which is used to elicit participants' views in a way which means they are 'owned' by the whole group is brainstorming. It encourages the free expression of pent-up resentments and the voicing of hitherto unexpressed views because people can say whatever comes to mind without having to weigh it for acceptability or polish it as a speech. Brainstorming consists of posing a straightforward question or topic to the group and recording on a board or a large sheet of paper all the responses which are forthcoming so that everyone present can see what is being written. There is no discussion of the ideas as they are recorded; group members simply state or shout out their own immediate reactions, for a set period of time or until they have nothing left to say. They are discouraged from reacting to or discussing other people's ideas at this stage.

The second stage of the exercise is to discuss all the points which members have listed in a way which searches for linking themes and common threads, so that what at first looks like a jumble of ideas begins to take on a definable shape. Group members are encouraged to express and compare their own opinions and experiences; these are not filtered out by the workers on the basis either of their own views or of differences they perceive between members in terms of age, status, or the ability to shout most loudly or articulate most clearly.

The skills required by the workers during a brainstorming exercise include those of eliciting comments, recording them accurately but succinctly, and drawing out what is only hesitantly forthcoming. It may be useful for one or more of the workers to sit amongst the group and to pick up any 'mutterings' so as to be able to encourage the most reticent to participate. As groups develop, participants themselves will be able to act as questioners or recorders of ideas, and some will be able to do this straightaway. This will usually be at the expense of that person's contribution to the ideas which are forthcoming, however, since they will be too busy to join in. Ideally, both recording of ideas and sorting them into themes should be done on large sheets of paper, or copied out if initially written up on a board, so that the group has a permanent record of its work and can return to its original concerns at a later date.

As well as finding out what everyone thinks, there are other reasons why brainstorming is a very useful technique at the earliest stages of a group. Individual members can contribute without being too much in the spotlight (people are looking at what is being written rather than staring at the speaker) which assists everyone to feel at home in the group and has the effect of drawing them together. It helps, firstly, if all those present suspend judgement on ideas proffered, with no criticism; secondly, if no limits are placed on the types of ideas which can be put forward – often the 'strangest' ones can lead the group in new and rewarding directions; thirdly, if as many ideas as possible can be gathered, the more the better; and, fourthly, if the ideas are imaginatively combined and contrasted in the second stage of the brainstorm.

A simple framework for forward planning can be introduced into a brainstorm, for example on the basis of 'likes' and 'dislikes'. This was done with a group of young people who constantly got into trouble with the police because they were bored and spent time hanging around on the streets. The groupworkers put a sheet of paper on the wall of the school dining-hall where the group had negotiated a venue for its initial meeting. After discussion over refreshments, the workers wrote two headings: 'good things' and 'bad things', referring to the housing estate where the young people all lived. This prompted talk about what there was to do locally and about the attitudes of local people towards group members. Ideas did not flow quickly to start with but, with a little prompting, a list emerged:

BAD	**GOOD**
Nothing to do	Swimming pool
Boredom	Chip shop
Schools	Laughs with mates
Police	
No open space to use	
Lack of respect	
Banned from using swimming pool	

The young people then came up with several ideas on how to improve such things as facilities, lack of respect, and the swimming pool ban. There and then, they decided to meet weekly to plan a campaign for their own youth club. Their immediate request was for a meeting-place of their own – off the streets – where they could play games, listen to music, drink coffee and generally atttempt to avoid conflict with adults which, in their view, had created trouble, offences and court appearances in the past. For the next week they all planned to walk round the estate to look at the facilities and places mentioned. Two years later, after a long period of hard work – including campaigning, petitions, discussions with senior police officers and elected councillors, forming a committee, and fund-raising - they got their club.

Clearly, this exercise is only one example of how to ask the question *'WHAT?'* It is one way of breaking the ice and building the group's identity whilst all the time focusing on participants' lived experience. It gets straight to the heart of what most concerns group members and, consequently, keeps the emphasis on their own words, priorities and choices. In this way, the exercise – the posing of the question – emphasises participation and empowers members to move onto the next stages in the group. The workers are facilitators and enablers of the activities and the discussion. They do not impose their own topics or insert their own ideas. Every single group member is involved and the workers' skill can be used in drawing everyone in: ensuring that quieter members – such as women or girls in mixed gender groups, someone who stammers or who mentions the things others would like to ignore – are not overlooked or rejected by the rest of the group. The workers also need to select exercises which match the abilities of the group, without underestimating anyone, and which catch members' interest.

Asking the Question '*WHY?*'

Working with group members to analyse *WHY?* the issues they have identified exist is the distinctive feature of practice which seeks to achieve empowerment. Without it, there can be no awareness of wider-scale oppression, no moving beyond members blaming themselves for their problems into greater awareness or the pursuit of social change. To jump straight from identifying *WHAT?* is wrong into the practicalities (the *HOW?*) of achieving change would be to collude with a process in which explanations of the responsibility for problems are usually sought in the private world around individual and family, either because this is the extent of the worker's own understanding or because it appears to them to make intervention more feasible. To ask the question '*WHY?*' brings social issues into play and opens up new options for action in the public world. It represents the application of the values of empowerment in practice.

One of the most clearly appropriate techniques to use in empowering groups, and one which tends to lead automatically from *WHAT?* into *WHY?* is consciousness-raising. In the early stages of the women's movement, members of consciousness-raising groups would sit in a circle and speak in turn about the everyday circumstances and events of their lives. No one in the group remained silent; no one interrupted or passed comment. This made it possible to share things which would have seemed inconsequential or wrong-headed in other, notably male, company. Women slowly learned to recognise and to value their own and each other's experiences (see Principle 1 above) and, in turn, to voice these more freely (see Principle 2). Gradually, it emerged that women had in common the same feelings of drudgery, duty, guilt, inadequacy and anger at housework, sole responsibility for child-rearing, and being taken for granted or abused by men. Issues that individuals had not previously even recognised as such – like who performed basic chores in the home, or how men assumed women to be stupid and unreliable – were heard repeatedly until the conclusion became inescapable that they affected all women, from all backgrounds, and could not be attributable any longer to individual failings on the part of those particular women. It was the fundamental relationships between men and women in society and in relationships, and women's consequent valuation of themselves (absorbed from men), which needed to change.

The Braunstone Women's Self-Help and Action Group went through all these stages of development. It was started by two social workers who were keen to work with women members in their own right as women, rather than through their relationship to the social services department as mothers, carers and clients – filed as 'child care' cases. Previous social workers had sought the women out individually to discuss all the things that seemed to go wrong in their daily lives and which

134

tended to make them feel like failures. At first, the women attending the group talked about themselves and their experiences. It was not long before each found that other women faced the same problems. Realising that the company of other women could be not only inspirational but uplifting, they built new friendship and support networks through the group which, as well as relieving isolation, fostered self-confidence, self-esteem and self-awareness.

As they began to see that other women had the same kinds of problems and obstacles to their development, the group members gradually began to recognise the general social oppression of all women and their own potential power and ability to gain control over their lives. They found this whole process of achieving new forms of understanding a revelation. As Lorna, one of the group members, put it: 'It's just amazing that someone else is saying the same as happened to you - it's a really unbelievable experience and instantly brings you out of yourself.' Another group member said: 'You know that you're no longer on your own, that others feel the same way – that you're not mad, or, if you are, so is everyone' (Wright, 1985, p.82). To take just one example, after sharing the pain and degra- dation of account after account of domestic abuse which relatives, friends and previous social workers had told each woman she must have provoked, the reali- sation now dawned on them that 'if you, you and you are battered, it can't be your faults'. After a time, then, the women in the group began to see that problems so common and widespread must have wider causes. The explanation of domestic violence begins to move away from one which 'blames the victim' (Ryan, 1971) to one which identifies a wider system of oppression of women by men in society. Campbell (1984, p.93) is clear that:

> *domestic violence . . . is something men do to women, not because they're mad or homicidal maniacs, but as an expression of ordinary domestic conflict between unequals. The violence is only the exercise of an ultimate weapon available to men.*

Longres and McLeod (1980, p.275) summarise, from their own experience in groupwork, the three stages of consciousness-raising through which this recogni- tion, or movement from *WHAT?* to *WHY?* happens:

> *themes generally surfaced as a private trouble experienced by an individual participant. As the discussions proceeded, however, attention shifted to the related experiences of others in the group, and then to the analysis of the structural sources of the shared troubles.*

The role for groupworkers in asking the question *'WHY?'* is to see that topics come from the group and are kept in play long enough for broader understanding to develop. This fosters a process of mutual learning among group members. It means threading a way through the maze of information, experience and feelings which all participants bring, in order to find broad themes and to keep the flow of discussion and action going (Lovett *et al.* 1983, p.82). The ideas which were forthcoming during the *'WHAT?'* stage should now be handed back to the group in a 'problem-posing' way (Freire, 1972), in order for the group to gain more awareness of the total issue. Prompts can be used in the ensuing discussion through a series of questions such as:

(a) Description   -   *What do you see happening?*
(b) Analysis   -   *Why is it happening?*
(c) Related problems   -   *What problems does it lead to?*
(d) Root Causes   -   *What are the causes of these problems?*

(Based on Hope and Timmel, 1984, p.60)

Asking the Question *'HOW?'*
After reaching an understanding of problems and their causes, the next stage for the group will be to move on to action planning, which consists of asking: *How can we do something about it?*

Longres and McLeod (1980, p.268) are clear that consciousness raising must go beyond increased understanding into action: 'reflection in search of understanding dehumanizing social structures . . . . [and] . . . action aimed at altering societal conditions. The two must go hand in hand; action without reflection is as unjustifiable as reflection without action.' This is what the present author understands by empowerment. In the North Braunstone women's group, reflection led to action both at the individual level, through an increasing ability to be assertive - Di began to expect her partner to take his turn at looking after their children, while Janet found the confidence to tell hers to leave - and at the wider level, with the women taking part in campaigns and conferences and eventually establishing their own women's centre.

Following the process of identification *(WHAT?)* and analysis *(WHY?)* of issues which the group wants to work on, feasibility exercises can be used to plan the specific action the group can undertake. Thus, the question *HOW?* is asked by breaking down the issues into component parts which are comprehensible and manageable, and which can be allocated as specific tasks. One way to do this is through the use of action grids. The various tasks can be plotted onto a grid in order to identify short-term, medium-term and longer-term goals, and to determine whether additional help will be required to meet them.

Other decisions facing the group can be plotted in a similar way, for example onto a 'resources grid' where the specifics of resources the group will need rather than tasks to be performed can be explored.

	Now	Soon	Later
By us			
With help			
By others			

A force-field analysis can also be used to identify possible ways forward for a group. It is based on the idea that the *status quo* is a relatively fragile balance held in place by pressure from two opposing directions. If, for example, one faction in a nation wants tight central control of the economy and another wants complete freedom of enterprise, if they are forced to share power the nation might end up neither at one pole nor the other but with relatively free trading overseen by a system of checks and safeguards. The force-field model of stasis and change has the advantage of greater flexibility in action planning since a group may decide either to strengthen the forces supporting its desired change or to weaken the restraining or opposing forces, or to do both. In most social work practice, only the first of these alternatives is actively considered as workers push, heads down, towards what they want to see happen. The force-field exercise opens up more options, is therefore more effective, and also makes it possible to consider whether strong or rapid movement in one direction will cause a backlash in the other. Possible actions can be considered in the light of detailed questions such as:

- What is it feasible for us to do as things stand?
- Which opposing forces are weakest and easiest to tackle?
- Which potential alliances are strongest?
- What are others doing?
- Where can both positive and negative forces be tackled at the same time?

Clearly there is potential for organising on a grid the tasks thus identified.

An example of a group reducing the opposition to its progress whilst also strengthening its wider supports can be seen in a self-advocacy group formed of adults with learning difficulties. It built on positives by publishing its own magazine, whilst opposing negatives by writing to complain to every television channel and newspaper that employed harmful stereotypes of people with learning difficulties. Letters were also sent in praise of positive images. Negative attitudes and decisions were further opposed by seeking representation on committees making decisions about the allocation of social services money; any proposals which were felt to restrict the lives of service users, to maintain their low social status, or to compound their lack of dignity and freedom of choice were voted against by the representatives. At the same time, positive options were increased by establishing a resource and drop-in centre independent of the local authority which made no distinctions on the grounds of educational achievements or background in institutional care. It mounted conferences at which people who had endured a lifetime of negative labelling could speak out about their concerns and aspirations. One of these was the first national conference in Britain for women with learning difficulties. Many activities combined opposition to negative forces with the promotion of positives. Running training days for professionals, for example, confronted the adverse and limiting attitudes perpetuated by powerful groups whilst, at the same time, building confidence, skills and self-esteem in group members who had hitherto lacked power. Gradually, their influence spread so that they are now routinely consulted in relation to health and welfare planning locally and are part of a national network of self-advocacy groups working to change the image and rights of disabled people.

Conclusion

Introducing the questions *'WHAT?'*, *'WHY?'* and *'HOW?'* consistently widens the areas of concern and potential action that service users will identify and hence can make a major difference to the work of every social worker. It can extend to external forces their view of the relevant and the possible. At the same time, it remains essential for groupworkers to challenge themselves and the groups with whom they work, to consider their emerging analyses and plans in the light of the overall practice principles of self-directed groupwork. These include the commitment to confronting oppression which means that some potential answers to *'HOW?'* are favoured over others. Thus, for example, solutions which empower one group at the expense of the oppression of another are not acceptable.

The way that self-directed understanding and action can unfold, moving out from personal problems to give access to public issues, can be encapsulated in a final practice example. A group for parents of children with learning difficulties which had been started by one hospital social worker with the intention of helping the parents to come to terms with their feelings of loss, anger and grief at having had a disabled child, was taken over by a second worker who as well as valuing those aspects of the work, gave the members more opportunity to voice their own grievances. She did not direct them back to their emotional reactions once their initial 'coming to terms' had occurred, but allowed their opinions on a range of issues to emerge by asking open-ended questions such as 'What is the worst thing now?' and 'Why is it like it is?' Gradually, the parents turned of their own accord to issues about lack of resources, and the way they had been treated. They subsequently put pressure on the local hospital to provide more short-term care beds, and they also gingered up a local voluntary group by involving it in campaigning to change medical practices, health policies and gaps in resources which sometimes led to the birth of brain-damaged children. Through their participation in the group, they were empowered to seek and to achieve change in organisations far bigger and more powerful than themselves. Their initial stimulus was personal pain, but their impact was public and empowering.

References
Campbell, B. (1984) *Wigan Pier Revisited: Poverty and Politics in the Eighties*, London: Virago.

Dobash, R. E. and Dobash, R. P. (1992) *Women, Violence and Social Change*, London: Routledge.

Freire, P. (1972) *Pedagogy of the Oppressed*, Harmondsworth: Penguin.

Hope, A. and Timmel, S. (1984) *Training for Transformation.* Gweru, Zimbabwe: Mambo Press.

Longres, J. F. and McLeod, E. (1980) 'Consciousness raising and social work practice', *Social Casework*, May, pp.267-276.

Lovett, T.; Clarke, C. and Kilmurray, A. (1983) *Adult Education and Community Action: Adult Education and Popular Social Movements*, London: Croom Helm.

Mullender, A. and Ward, D. (1985) 'Towards an alternative model of social groupwork', *British Journal of Social Work, 15, pp.155-172.*

Mullender, A. and Ward, D. (1989) 'Challenging familiar assumptions: preparing for and initiating a self-directed group', *Groupwork*, 2(1), pp.5-26.

Mullender, A. and Ward, D. (1991) *Self-Directed Groupwork: Users Take Action for Empowerment*, London: Whiting and Birch.

Mullender, A. and Ward, D. (1993) 'The Role of the Consultant in Self-Directed Group Work: an Approach to Supporting Social Action in Britain', *Social Work with Groups*, 16(4), pp.57-79.

Ryan, W. (1971) *Blaming the Victim* , London: Orbach and Chambers.

Ward, D. and Mullender, A. (1991) 'Facilitation in self-directed groupwork', *Groupwork,* 4(2), pp.141-151.

Wright, M. (1985) 'Mirror of a womens group' in Landau-North, M. and Duddy, S. (eds.) *Self-Help Through the Looking Glass*, Leicester: Leicester Council for Voluntary Service.

Empowerment and Practice: Community Development Work with Vietnamese People

Jill Reynolds

Summary

This chapter looks at the work of Vietnamese community development workers in stimulating the community participation of Vietnamese people settled in England and Wales. Refugees from Vietnam were dispersed in resettlement, often at some distance from their compatriots. The community development workers aim to build strong communities capable of full participation in UK society, and to improve the quality of response to community need from statutory and voluntary services.

The chapter describes how the workers go about meeting people and assisting them to form associations. Friendship, shared culture and shared refugee experience are amongst the resources the Vietnamese workers bring to relationships in facilitating community development. They build the confidence of people who are apprehensive about their ability to take a lead in the community. A friendly, supportive and encouraging approach is often also needed to empower service providers, who may lack confidence in working with refugees.

The problems and possibilities for encouraging participation are explored. The pace of change has to be seen in the context of people who have mostly been in the UK for less than fifteen years, who have been separated from close or extended family networks, and who are learning about unfamiliar UK systems.

Community development work is about the active involvement of people in the issues which affect their lives. It aims to develop their skills and experience in responding to these issues, and give opportunities for genuine participation (Standing Conference on Community Development, 1993). Empowerment, in the sense of increasing people's control over decisions affecting their lives, is thus a fundamental principle of community development work. This chapter explores the potential and the problems in seeking to empower people from Vietnam living in the UK, through community development.

Over the last ten years a voluntary agency called Refugee Action has had a team of workers engaged in community development with Vietnamese people settled in the UK. The overall aims are:

- to enable refugees from Vietnam to be self-sufficient and able to participate fully in UK society whilst retaining their cultural identity and

- to ensure better service provision for Vietnam refugees.

This article draws on interviews I held with Refugee Action workers. At the time of my interviews the community development team numbered fifteen in all. The workers are based in four different cities, and are often some distance from the regions of England and Wales which they cover. For instance, the worker for the south of England is based in London, and his region stretches some 150 miles from Wiltshire in the west to Essex in the east. However, workers plan their goals and strategies for each year and may select particular locations which can benefit from their support.

Regional Development Workers might be working with Vietnamese settled in an area to set up a community group, or to establish the kind of organisational structure which could enable them to plan and carry out activities. They also make contact with statutory and voluntary bodies in the locality to develop their awareness of the needs of refugees and encourage the provision of better services. The team has national advisers who have specific briefs, for instance in relation to stimulating community provision for women, setting up employment projects, or helping community groups acquire management skills. Two team co-ordinators have a managerial role in assisting team members to plan and achieve their goals.

In 1993 and 1994 I interviewed eight of Refugee Action's Vietnamese workers and managers and the two white British community development team co-ordinators. I also spoke to some locally employed Vietnamese community workers and community group members. My own link with the team was through having worked for the organisation ten years earlier, when I had supervised Vietnamese social work fieldworkers in their initial resettlement support to Vietnamese refugees. As a white, British academic teaching about health and social care roles I was interested in learning more about the current team's work and wanted to examine the ways in which they sought to 'empower' Vietnamese settlers.

What community?
The community development workers seek to build strong communities, as a basis for enabling Vietnamese people to participate fully in UK society. In a 'statement of purpose' they hold themselves accountable to 'the Vietnamese community'. Yet this community does not exist as a single identifiable grouping.

What community do Vietnamese people belong to? People did not arrive in Britain with their families and networks intact. They came from a country which had long been embroiled in war, and with continuing divisions between those from the north and those from the south, as well as differences in language and ethnicity between the ethnic Chinese and ethnic Vietnamese. There is also a question regarding the point at which people who arrived as refugees from Vietnam, having achieved UK citizenship, may define their community as wider than simply that of expatriates.

Of the 26,000 people of Vietnamese origin now living in the UK approximately half are living in London. Outside London and the larger cities the Vietnamese population is quite scattered with low numbers in any one town. This is deliberate, due to a policy of dispersal in the 1970s and 1980s when the bulk of Vietnamese people arrived. It was thought then that large collections of refugees might result in racist responses, and it was also a way of spreading the load regarding housing and other services which would mean that special housing provision need not be made.

The dispersal policy has not been helpful for community development purposes. However, in spite of the difficulties for such scattered groupings, over the fifteen years of settlement in the UK Vietnamese people have set up more than forty community associations. Many of these associations have been able to get local authority or other funding support to employ community workers and advise workers: in 1991 there were forty funded posts within London and a further thirty outside London. These posts are in the main filled by Vietnamese workers. Refugee Action has given some support and co-ordination to the developing community groups. Its main involvement in community development is outside London, in those areas where community groups are either non-existent or still quite weak. One of the concerns of the community development team is to ensure that membership of the developing community groups aims at being as inclusive as possible, embracing cultural, ethnic and other divisions. It is less easy to influence established groups.

It may not be obvious to Vietnamese people living in a small, suburban town that, together with others in the same county or region who originate from Vietnam, they form a community. In areas where there are only four or five families in the town, forming a community association may not be an option. Some people have been successful at maintaining their own culture while forming friendships with local British people. However, difficulties in communicating across a language barrier mean that most people are likely to experience extreme isolation in their early days of settlement. This can provide the motivation for getting together with others from Vietnam. But developing such community links is not a process which happens without some determined leadership or some outside assistance, such as Refugee Action's community development team has offered.

Self-sufficiency

Refugee Action's strategy has been to encourage self-help through the development of community associations which can set up groups, clubs and some services; for instance for young people, for women, mother-tongue classes for children, lunch clubs for older people. However, the aim of 'self-sufficiency' is a concept which is hard to pin down. Self-sufficiency can contain an implication that people should pull themselves up by their own bootstraps, not make demands on others. There have often been erroneous assumptions about newcomers to Britain, particularly regarding people of Asian origin, that all social and welfare needs can be met from within the ethnic group (Gunaratnam, 1993). Yet full participation in UK society must mean that people have the same rights, and therefore the same opportunities to use services as any citizen. Such participation is obviously difficult to effect for people who are unfamiliar with British systems and traditions, and unable to speak much English, especially when they come from a country which has no strong historical ties with the UK. Community associations may provide a way for people to deal with some of their own social, cultural and welfare needs, and to articulate these needs more clearly to service providers.

Refugee Action's workers have not seen better service provision for Vietnamese people and self-sufficiency as contradictory aims. One of the community development team co-ordinators emphasised that helping the community to organise and set up strongly managed groups had to be done in parallel with raising awareness of needs amongst service providers. Where the worker did not work closely with agencies, but just concentrated on the community, it had not been very productive. Building a strong community association, able to fulfil some social and welfare functions, was, she thought, a good long term aim, but not one achievable in all areas. Sometimes it was appropriate to work more on broadening out existing local services. For instance, the numbers of Vietnamese people in an area might mean that a separate Vietnamese lunch club for older people was not a practicality, but work could be done with local social services to make sure that lunch clubs included Vietnamese foods, and made people feel more welcome.

A Vietnamese senior manager also endorsed the need to link up the Vietnamese groups with service providers and other community groups:

> *In some areas they still keep to their own, and are very isolated, and I don't think that's the right way to do it. They have to work with other people, have contact with local authorities, or other community groups and ethnic minorities.*

These twin tasks of helping communities to organise and raising awareness amongst local agencies have been central to the work of the community development team. I look now at how the community development workers actually went about this work.

Helping communities to organise
Getting started

A number of the community development workers in the regions had spent a good deal of time in making contact with individuals and families in different areas. They talked to as many people as possible, often making more than one visit to get to know a family, and find out how they were faring. In areas where there were few previous links, they might start by looking through the phone book for Vietnamese names. At each household they would ask about other families to visit. They would deliberately cast the net as widely as possible. In time they would talk about possibilities for forming a community group. A shared cultural background and an understanding of the time needed to build up friendship and trust were important:

> *You make some kind of friendship, build up some friendship with them, and then on the second or third visit, talk about the difficulty they face, and the benefit an organised group can bring to them.*

This facility of Vietnamese workers to engage more effectively by 'coming as a friend' was identified in some early work done by Vietnamese people trained as social work fieldworkers (Bang, 1983). It seems to be equally important in community development.

Voluntary involvement in community activity appears to have been unfamiliar in Vietnam, where helping activity was more likely to be organised around family ties. Sometimes the development workers appealed to some sense of shared difficulties and experiences to persuade people of the usefulness of working on issues collectively. One worker referred to his own experience of feeling downcast when refused for educational courses. He said:

> *I use my own experience when I talk to other Vietnamese people. I say 'Hey, the only way we can work together, help together, is if we join up as a community, that's all. That's the only way we can survive. Don't worry about whether you come from the north or the south'.*

The community development workers thought that some of the divisions between different groups, while not completely buried, were being coped with differently because of the need for some solidarity. One person referred to a Vietnamese proverb:

'The bedfellows have different dreams': the same bed, but different dreams. That means they still keep their feelings there, but they do not show them because they must join each other.

In addition to advocating mutual support, some thought that a tradition of keeping personal and family problems private also needed challenging:

I always have to explain to them 'speak out, don't isolate yourself'. Because people don't talk about problems. A lot of things are happening now, like children running away from home, a lot of things are kept inside the community, inside the family.

The community development workers were conscious that they were trying to persuade people of the benefits of joining together at a time when many people were still very needy and encountering personal difficulties in their settlement. Often in the initial stages of making contact with people the workers had to be prepared to offer support over personal problems to individuals and families.

Keeping things going
The difficulties that groups went through in their early stages are not dissimilar to those that any voluntary groups suffer (see for example Henderson and Thomas, 1987). People might express interest in having a Vietnamese class for the children, for instance, but when it came to calling a meeting, did not attend. Personalities sometimes clashed. The motivation for involvement on a committee might be mainly for the status it could bring, so that members were then unprepared to take on actual tasks. Younger members were often too busy studying or looking for work to spare time to work for their community.

The community development workers accepted that groups needed time to develop, and gave sensitive support to this process. One worker tried to build up trust between a treasurer and chair who 'did not agree on anything - even who will sign the cheque!' He found

You spend a lot of energy just on silly things. Sometimes they've got a very strong inferiority complex. One person says something, the other person thinks differently. So you have to study, try to make peace between them.

It took a year to make things better between them. I do not say it feels easy, but they talk now.

In another area he found that lack of trust between group members made it quite difficult for them to organise anything together, but with support from himself they started to become more effective. He showed that he was willing to work with them on an activity that they thought they could handle:

Among themselves they are so weak. They haven't got enough people to work together with them. All that they could manage was to organise a Christmas party. When they saw that I could help them with the first step they started to believe that they could trust me, and work together with me, towards proper ends. So we held a general meeting and we sat down to plan activities. Then we got an office, a temporary one. We use it only once a week because they haven't got a paid worker, volunteers do it.

Learning from earlier experience that people without genuine commitment often put themselves forward for committee roles, he was careful to be inclusive in starting up another group:

I said, 'We'll go round to get ideas from each person, so that everyone has a say'. And I encouraged them to talk, and we started to build up the community work. The management group is eight: one is disabled, two women, one elderly, so it's very, very good. The member for the elderly, she's elderly herself, that's good.

This worker was aiming to include a range of people in the management group and to be sure that disadvantaged people had opportunities to participate. It was obvious from talking to workers that they had learnt from each other over a number of years different techniques for resolving disputes; to draw out people who might normally speak little in groups; and to give people confidence in themselves.

Building up confidence
Engaging Vietnamese community members and encouraging their continuing participation required a lot of positive valuing of their contributions, and nurturing of abilities. One development worker described the work he was doing with some older community members. They could not communicate with local people so were interested in being actively involved in the community association:

You can imagine, they came without language, they came without knowledge, they came without British qualifications. They came without confidence. They were the most difficult people to work with, because they'd got an inferiority complex. You have to build their confidence. They want to take part in the group, but they're not sure about their roles: whether they could be the chair.

In this area, the association was fortunate in having some very positive support from local health and social services agencies.

Gradually, with the help of community development workers and helpful responses from local agencies, confidence could be built up. This detailed attention to what people need in order to be able to participate effectively illustrates the time needed and the work involved in seeking to empower people to take on unfamiliar tasks.

Training and information

The business of keeping community activities going requires skills in organisation, planning, fund-raising and budgeting. Even quite modest ventures need a place to meet, and this often has costs. As groups become more established, they may want to be able to undertake projects and to pay a worker to nurture new projects and take on some of the administrative work. They need skills then in applying for funding and if they are successful they need skills in managing paid workers.

As well as giving individual help to groups in getting started, Refugee Action has organised regional 'skill-sharing' meetings, where committee members can learn about the roles of chair, secretary, treasurer and so on, and should they reach the point of appointing staff, acquire skills in managing workers. In this way new committee members can be inducted into what is involved. The community groups management adviser indicated the problems:

> *They are volunteers, they change every year. In Vietnam, we haven't got these kind of committees and associations, so in this country we learn how to set up the management committee, and try to learn how to run. There are so many problems, because the knowledge, the skill, the time. . . . When the committee has got the funding, they find it difficult to get the funding, but when they find the funding, they have a worker, so they have to manage the worker, yes more problems.*

A handbook for Vietnamese community associations Methods for Managing (Ung and Graessle, 1990) gives valuable information and advice on setting up committees, and the skill-sharing meetings draw on this book in exploring needs and difficulties.

Offering opportunities to acquire committee skills is a useful resource. The handbook is very clear on the need to take account of all groups in the community, ensuring that women and younger people are encouraged to join the committee. It warns of the dangers of one person, often the chair, doing all the work, holding all the power, and running out of energy. These are the sorts of issues which skill-sharing meetings grapple with too. Such notions of community empowerment and participation seem to be at odds with people's previous conceptions of how things get done. One worker described the different tradition in Vietnam:

> *We didn't have this type of voluntary group at home. We just had the admin-istrative work, the hierarchy from province to hamlet. But we did not have much of the voluntary organisations like this in which you can make a move for the people to participate fully in the community. So people are confused from there. When people sit on the management committee they feel it is like a position in the administration. But it is much more difficult.*

People are inducted into a traditional committee mode, which can be quite hierar-chical, while at the same time an ethos of equality and participation is promoted. Acquiring skills in both areas at once is quite a sophisticated undertaking.

Is an introduction to a form of committee procedures which accords with British cultural traditions empowering or disempowering? It could be argued that this is actually akin to imposing an alien form on Vietnamese groups. However, without some structures which are recognisable in a British context, Vietnamese groups would be unlikely to get access to the range of resources they have been success-ful in tapping. Offering information and help in acquiring committee skills means that groups have a choice in relation to procedures. They can decide not to use this committee mode, or adapt it to suit their purposes.

Workers and committees
Helping groups to achieve an effective balance between the paid workers and the volunteer management committees is an important area. Without training, workers can find that they are having to induct new committee members into their roles, or an over-controlling committee may keep the worker on such a tight rein that he or she is unable to make a creative contribution. Committees have to learn how to be responsible employers, and the demand this places on people's time can be quite a commitment. There are parallels in other self-help initiatives: for instance in relation to mental health self-advocacy projects things can go so badly wrong that groups lose sight of their original purposes, and people experience a sense of personal failure (Wallcraft, 1994).

Those committee members who have time for their roles may be unemployed themselves, and resent the worker's privilege of paid employment. For the indi-vidual committee member the benefits of participation in community affairs have to be balanced against the lack of financial reward and possible out-of-pocket expenses. With this in mind, Refugee Action give assistance towards travel and other costs to enable people to attend skill-sharing meetings.

Simply finding the time to go to a skill-sharing meeting is a problem for many. One worker employed by her community association in London found it hard to persuade her committee to go to outside training in committee roles, but tried to do something herself that would help them work as a team, for one or two days each year, collectively with the committee:

> *Last year we had a meeting in Paris! That way they also want to go. I say 'You want to go for your holiday, why don't we go together, we'll pay for ourselves, but after that we get a chance to see each other' They agreed, so it's lovely.*

This kind of strategy, which involved the community worker in using her holiday on community organisation matters, gives the flavour of the personal investment that the Vietnamese workers tended to have in building strong communities. As an outsider, I was concerned that this worker had a demanding job in an area of high deprivation. She would have needs herself for support, but in order to get this from committee members she first had to help them to work as a team. The merging of personal and working life did not appear to be experienced as a burden by this particular worker.

The potential for friendship seemed in general to be central to workers' effectiveness in encouraging people to get involved in community action. However, it could lead to problems, and some of the regional development workers were struggling to scale down the high demands that they were placed under to get involved in their local community affairs in their own time. The team co-ordinators were aware of these pressures, and used evaluation sessions with development workers to help them find the right balance for themselves between over-involvement and distance.

The community development workers took on many different roles with the Vietnamese settlers in enabling them to become involved in community activity. They acted as facilitators and often mediators in bringing people together and sorting out squabbles. In this, an approach involving friendship, combined with enough impartiality to achieve widespread trust, was important. They provided leadership, which took into account the goals and aspirations of the Vietnamese people in the region. They coached and encouraged people to express their views, and became trainers in committee and management skills.

The work that the community development workers did to raise awareness and improve skills amongst local agencies and service providers, although very different, involved them in many similar roles.

Raising awareness amongst local agencies

Community development workers had various strategies for opening discussions with local agencies. Since they did not usually have a local base, they had to gain some credibility initially. One person would find out from looking at mail the Vietnamese families received whether any discussions or conferences were taking place that might be relevant. He would attend, sometimes taking a family with him, and raise issues affecting the Vietnamese settlers. Another worker adopted a higher profile approach. He would talk to individuals, sympathetic people in the local authority or workers in the Council for Race Equality, find out who else might be helpful at this point, and sow the seeds for bringing service providers together for a conference on the needs of the Vietnamese. Yet another strategy used by several people was to ask for representatives from local service providers and potential funding bodies to act as a support group for Vietnamese community association committees.

Often the community development workers found that local authorities were very ignorant of the existence of Vietnamese people in the area. At one social service committee a request for funding met with a stream of racist questions such as: 'Why, if the Vietnamese came to this country more than ten years ago, do they still not speak English?' 'Why, since they have not asked for anything in all this time, do they now ask for money?' 'Does the British government continue to receive Vietnamese refugees? If so, when will we have a "Vietnamese town", because at the moment we have a Chinatown already?'

When a more sympathetic response was received, development workers would take a supportive and coaching role in preparing Vietnamese committees to address meetings of service providers themselves:

> *I want to build their confidence. I let them know I am there. 'If you do not speak clearly, you cannot express yourself, just say it in Vietnamese. Do not worry, I will interpret for you'.*

However, forging links and raising awareness were not enough. Community development workers had a continuing role in giving support and coaching to the social service or health workers who might become involved in helping individuals and families. There might be problems in finding an interpreter, or training needed to alert people to hidden problems. Development workers recognised that morale was often quite low in local authority offices. One person found that he spent a long time on the telephone lending a sympathetic ear to harassed social services and health workers. He talked about the need to empower social workers to tackle this new area of work in similar terms to the way he had spoken of the needs of Vietnamese people: building up confidence, giving them good feedback, 'make people feel happy, enjoy the work'. It appeared he found it almost as important to build some kind of friendship with the social services workers as it was with potential community activists.

The willingness and ability of local agencies to engage with the needs and problems of the Vietnamese in their areas sometimes ran ahead of the capacities of the community associations, and sometimes lagged far behind. The development workers could not always achieve a perfect match, but by putting effort into building links between Vietnamese people and local agencies, they created the possibility that some mutual understanding would emerge.

Can you make communities share power?
The community development team's role was essentially facilitative. They could help communities get started, draw in more people, build up confidence, and establish links with local agencies. They could try to persuade people that it was worthwhile and enjoyable to take part in community activities. They saw this as part of the process of offering people choices. One person spoke of the need to 'empower people so that they know what they want'. The picture that community workers gave me was of many Vietnamese people so cut off from sources of information or understanding of possibilities in the UK that without the lifeline from a community association they would have had very little chance of participating in any sense in UK society.

The community development workers were enthusiastic about extending opportunities and treating people equally. In relation to ethnic and political differences, one person responded: 'I think that the best tool we have learnt in this country is about the equal opportunities'. He was concerned to engage people actively in their communities and give them access to decision-making at least at this level: 'Because if they do not participate, it means that a minority of people get control over things. It's not right at all.'

In the long run, however, the community association's ability to function effectively and be empowering of the wider Vietnamese community relies on the efforts of people living in the area, not on the development worker. The Refugee Action workers modelled an approach of sharing information and working in an inclusive way to involve as many people as possible. They could not be sure that community associations would continue to function in this way. As in any group, some people may simply like the status of holding office, and be ineffective in their roles, or they may take an autocratic approach and hold onto information in a way that makes others dependent on them.

For some community development workers there was frustration in the 'arm's length' nature of their role. They did not necessarily feel very powerful themselves. One person illustrated the difficulties by describing an interview process for a worker with one community association. He had found that principles of equal opportunity and confidentiality in interviewing were hard to get across to the management committee, and that the appointment they had made was not according to these principles. At the end of the day, he had to accept their choice: 'Provide advice, assist the group, you're like an assistant, you have no power.'

Conclusion
Success on the road to empowerment is hard to measure. Most Vietnamese people have been settled in the UK for less than fifteen years. The pace of community development is slow and it is not surprising that one team leader summed up the progress as: 'One step forward, two steps back.' People need time to make mistakes and learn from them as well as the more obvious successes of thriving community centres buzzing with activities. The strategies that have been used in community development are short term ones related to the current situation of Vietnamese people in the UK, finding ways of coping with limited access to mainstream services. A process has been set in motion however. In the longer term it is to be hoped that experience that Vietnamese people are gaining now in running their community associations, employing and managing workers, and opening up dialogue with local agencies will ease the way for fuller participation in UK society.

Empowerment is essentially a political strategy. It is a deliberate attempt to widen access to power. One of the paradoxes of empowerment as a strategy is that no one can really empower anyone else (Gomm, 1993). Opportunities can be improved, but ultimately people have to take power for themselves. They find their own ways of doing this. I was sometimes surprised at the low key approach to change that people were adopting. For instance, the development worker for women sees equality for women as a long term goal, involving the new generation of women brought up in the UK more than those who arrived as adults:

I think my job is really to reassure the whole community that setting up a women's self help group isn't going to make the marriage worse or anything. It just gives a woman a chance to do things for herself, you know, do a bit of training, not just doing housework and looking after children, they have time to do other things for themselves.

Rather than work directly on raising awareness or increasing assertiveness, she prefers to let things develop naturally: 'If they do a lot of things together it naturally gives them more confidence. In their own way, in their own time, they will become more assertive.'

The efforts of the community development team to empower Vietnamese communities illustrate a number of issues in this kind of work. The social isolation that many Vietnamese settlers encounter suggests that the maintenance of culture through community associations is a priority. But without strong links to British institutions and services, groups may struggle to survive, and individuals are not helped to participate in UK society. The community association's ability to be active, and local agencies' preparedness to be supportive will not always move at the same pace. Community development workers can act as bridges, and may need to give considerable attention to empowering the workers in health and social services so that they can give a more relevant service.

Encouraging people to be active in their communities is rarely easy: not everyone wants to be a community activist. Members of Vietnamese management committees are working to establish ways of managing functions, projects or people. The process may be quite unfamiliar to them, the complex of grants, applications and funding requirements bewildering. In the end, people may prefer to concentrate their energies on finding or keeping employment, or dealing with the personal demands of adapting to life in a new country. It is not very empowering when one person, whether committee member or paid worker, ends up having to take responsibility for everything, nor when groups break up because people cannot work effectively together. The community development workers can help people to acquire skills in committee and management tasks and learn how to work together. They can model an approach which involves sharing of power and information and increases the opportunities for people to participate. And sometimes the result is that a community comes into being where none was thought to exist.

References

Bang, S. (1983) *We Come as a Friend: Towards a Vietnamese Model of Social Work*, Derby: Refugee Action

Gomm, R. (1993) 'Issues of power in health and welfare' in Walmsley, J. Reynolds, J. Shakespeare, P. and Woolfe, R. (eds) *Health, Welfare and Practice: Reflecting on Roles and Relationships* London: Sage

Gunaratnam, Y. (1993) 'Breaking the silence: Asian carers in Britain' in Bornat, J.; Pereira, C.; Pilgrim, D. and Williams, F. (eds) *Community Care: a Reader* London: Macmillan

Henderson, P. and Thomas, D. (1987) *Skills in Neighbourhood Work* London: Allen and Unwin

Standing Conference on Community Development (1993) *Annual Report: Building for Change* (available from SCCD, 356, Glossop Road, Sheffield S10 2HW)

Ung, V. L. and Graessle, L. (1990) *Methods for Managing: a Handbook for Community Associations of Refugees from Vietnam* Derby: Refugee Action

Wallcraft, J. (1994) 'Empowering empowerment: professionals and self-advocacy projects' *Mental Health Nursing* 14 (2) 6-9

Family Therapy and Empowerment

John Carpenter

Summary

People's problems are often best understood in terms of their relationships with other important people in their lives, especially their families. Family therapy is a method of social work intervention in which family members come together to discuss their problems with a therapist. The emphasis is on change so that families can resolve their relationship problems and regain control over their lives. This chapter includes an example of family therapy and discusses how family therapy can, and cannot, be empowering.

What is family therapy?

Although social workers have worked with families since the beginning of this century, in activities such as counselling mothers on managing their children and providing support to family members in dealing with financial problems, in the late 1960s in the USA and the 1970s in Britain, many social workers become fascinated by new theories which conceptualised the family as a group or system. Together with colleagues from psychiatry, they began to develop ways of understanding and intervening with families. Bringing all the family members together in one room, whether they were the families of people with mental illness or families in which children were out of control of their parents, was quickly realised to have powerful effects. When families were encouraged to open up and talk together, terrific energy could be released. Simply asking people to give their different points of view on problems, and helping them to clarify what they are saying so that the message is heard by others in the family, may in itself lead to changes in attitudes and behaviour. This method came to be called 'family therapy'.

Family therapy is both an approach and a method. It is an approach to understanding people's psychological problems in terms of their relationships with others. An individual is always considered as a member of various social systems of which the family is usually, but not necessarily, the most significant. The family, in turn, is considered as a system in interaction with other systems, such as the neighbourhood, schools, work, and heath and welfare agencies. For this reason, some writers prefer to use the term 'systemic' to describe the approach and to differentiate it from the methods used which, when the focus is on the family group, is properly called family therapy.

It is usually individuals who are referred but family therapists typically assume that their 'client' is the family as a whole. An individual's symptoms or problems are seen as evidence of a family system in difficulty, a system that is not adapting to stress from within or from external pressures. The solution lies not in simply curing the presenting problem of the individual but in helping the family members to find new patterns of meaning and behaviour, with the most positive outcomes for all.

Method
The essential method of family therapy, therefore, is to bring members of the family together to discuss their problems. The role of the therapist is to facilitate this process. As in any method of social work or counselling, the relationship between the therapist and the family members is crucial. The ability to establish positive relationships (a process usually known as 'joining') is the most important aspect of the therapist's behaviour in determining the outcome of therapy. It is important to stress that joining is not just a matter for the beginning of therapy, but rather a process which requires attention throughout (Carpenter and Treacher, 1989).

In family therapy, the practitioner is required to be active, both to facilitate discussion and to intervene. Interventions are any specific actions which the therapist might take in order to promote change in the system. These include observations and interpretations of the family's behaviour as well as recommendations that family members should do certain 'tasks' both during and after the meeting. Interventions are designed to perturb the system, to help its members understand or experience things differently.

There are a large number of techniques used in family therapy, some of which are discussed in this chapter. These techniques are commonly associated with different 'schools' of family therapy which developed in the United States and western Europe over the last thirty years. The most influential schools have been structural family therapy (Minuchin, 1974), strategic, 'brief' therapy (Fisch, *et al.*, 1982; Haley, 1976) and the Milan Approach (Selvini Palazzoli *et al.*, 1978).

Where is family therapy practised?
In the United States and western Europe, family therapy is employed extensively in child and family guidance centres and psychiatric clinics. Psychiatrists and psychologists as well as social workers specialising in child and family problems work as therapists, often in pairs or teams. Working with colleagues is popular because the complexity of family problems and the emotional intensity of relationships are sometimes overwhelming, especially for inexperienced practitioners. Family therapy is also increasingly used to help adults with psychiatric problems,

including schizophrenia and adolescents with anorexia nervosa. In these cases, social workers work in close partnership with psychiatrists in hospitals and clinics.

In Britain and the United States, social workers employing a systemic approach to their work with children and families, including child protection, make a flexible use of family therapy methods. They must make a careful assessment of who is involved in the problem, and this might include friends and neighbours as well as members of the extended family. In the case of a child who is refusing to go to school, for example, if the problems appears to lie within the family, the therapist will work with the family group. But if the problem appears to lie between the family and the school, the social worker will bring together family members and school staff in order to resolve the difficulties. In a number of cases, both interventions will be appropriate.

Empowerment

The attraction of family therapy for many social workers is its active, change-promoting orientation. Family therapy is not about supporting clients in their difficulties (although a supportive relationship is a necessary factor for effective work) or even about ameliorating those difficulties. Rather, it is about change. The focus is on helping people to resolve their relationship problems and regain control over their lives - in short to 'empower people'. In contrast, providing support, especially long term support, would be seen as *dis*empowering in that it creates dependency on social workers and others. Merely ameliorating problems is similarly disempowering when it removes the pressure for change and resolution.

The very act of bringing the members of a family together to discuss their difficul-ties carries an important message about change and whose responsibility it is. If the problem is with a child, not only will the mother be expected to come, but the father also. If an adolescent is the focus of attention, the brothers and sisters will also be invited to the meetings where it will be explained that their contribution will be very important. If an elderly man's deteriorating mental health is the cause for concern, not only will the daughter or son with whom he is living be invited but his other children too, as well as neighbours and friends who may be willing to help. The message the family therapist is giving is: "You are the people who can resolve these problems. I can help, but it's down to you."

An example of family therapy

Maria, a young woman of twenty-three took an overdose. Fortunately, her mother found her unconscious on the kitchen floor and had her rushed to hospital where, after emergency treatment in the intensive care unit, her life was saved. When her

English mother and Spanish father visited her in hospital there was an enormous row as each blamed the other for what had happened to their only child. At one point, the nurses had to intervene to prevent them coming to blows. This incident was reported to the psychiatrist on duty in the hospital who then interviewed Maria.

The psychiatrist noted that Maria was suffering from feelings of failure, unworthiness, guilt and blame. She described a chaotic and argumentative atmosphere at home. The psychiatrist concluded that she should be referred to a social worker.

The social worker arranged to meet Maria with her parents. He listened carefully to what each of them had to say. Maria's problems seemed to be concerned with leaving home. This is always a key transition in the family life cycle, especially for an only child. She had first made the transition when she went away to university in another city and lived with other students. However, she had been very homesick and had often returned home when she felt lonely or under pressure. Her mother recalled how she had always welcomed her with open arms on these occasions. In spite of her difficulties, Maria graduated successfully and spent the next few months in Spain with her father's family, teaching English in a language school.

The real problem started when she returned home for the funeral of her aunt, her mother's only sister. She described how her mother had been very distressed and how she had decided to stay at home to give support. She maintained that her father had been grossly insensitive to her mother's grief. Nine months later Maria was still at home with no work and she rarely left the house. She described herself as miserable and useless. Just before she had tried to kill herself her mother had taken her to the doctor who had diagnosed depression and given her medicines.

Both parents had tried in their own ways to help Maria: her father with his shouts of "pull yourself together" and her mother with cosseting and protestations of love. They argued vociferously about her and the only positive thing about the situation was that Maria's problems had apparently pulled her mother out of her incapacitating grief.

Maria said very little during the first family meeting so, in order to explore issues that she seemed hesitant to express in front of her parents, the social worker saw her on her own. In the subsequent family meeting, the social worker helped Maria to share these ideas. Maria said that ever since she had been a child she had felt responsible for keeping the peace between her parents. She felt as if she was the parent and they were her argumentative children. She worried that her mother would be the victim of her father's violent temper and that her father would drive himself to a heart attack. When her aunt died, she knew that she was all her mother had and she knew, as a good Spanish girl, that it was her duty to look after them in their final years. The fact that they were continuing to argue made her feel that she had failed and because they were arguing about her, she felt that she was to blame for the rows. She reasoned that at least if she were dead they would have less reason to argue and might even reunite in their grief.

It was important during the family meeting for the social worker to support Maria in expressing her views and to prevent her parents dismissing her feelings or going back to blaming each other. Certainly, they were understandably upset about what had happened, but there was little point in trying to decide who, if anyone, was to blame. Instead, the social worker explained, they had a crucial task in helping their daughter to get things into perspective. They were invited to discuss their beliefs about family life and, in particular, their views on the relationships between mothers and daughters and parents and children. Is it inevitably a daughter's job to look after her parents?

Maria, they said, children are not responsible for their parents, even in Spain, until both are a good deal older. What is more, self-sacrifice is no answer. But, the social worker remarked, they shouldn't just expect Maria to take their assurances: they had to face the challenge of proving to Maria that they did not need her to supervise their relationship and that they could resolve their own differences. Yes, Maria's father agreed, Maria didn't seem to realise just what a struggle it had been for him and her mother when he had come to live in England. The social worker invited Maria's parents to tell their story: how her father had learnt English; how they had overcome the objections of her family to her marrying a foreigner; the joy of Maria's birth. They told how they had set up a business together which, in spite of difficult early years, was now flourishing. In telling this story they began to delight in their achievements; perhaps they hadn't been such failures after all.

Over the next few weeks, Maria's parents surprised her by showing considerable competence in sorting out their own affairs. Her father even went to the doctor to get a letter proving that he was in no danger of a heart attack. For a while, though, Maria still refused to go out. The social worker challenged her for using her parents as an excuse not to face the outside world. Maria accepted the challenge. She learnt to drive a car, joined a club and made friends. After a while, she got a job that reflected her qualifications and left home. Her parents did not, of course, kill each other when she had gone.

Comment

This necessarily brief account illustrates some key principles in empowering people through family therapy. First, as in all social work or therapy, the social worker tried to establish a positive relationship. In family therapy, this means a positive relationship with each member. The therapist's first task is to listen, to understand and to convey that understanding. When people feel understood, and not blamed, it is easier for them to change. In Maria's case, the therapist saw her separately for one meeting. This recognised her autonomy as a young woman with her own feelings and needs separate from her parents. It also forged an alliance with the therapist in which she could feel supported and empowered to explain her thoughts to her parents. In the subsequent family meeting, the therapist ensured that she had space to present her views.

On the foundation of this 'therapeutic alliance', the therapist challenged Maria's assumptions about family roles and responsibilities: was it inevitably a daughter's role to look after her parents? Maybe he was also challenging her parent's assumptions too. Whatever the case may have been, it was her parents (and not the therapist) who articulated a clear statement to their daughter; they felt empowered to act as parents.

Next, the therapist assumed their competence: if they were challenged to prove that they could survive without being overly dependent on each other, they could do it. They didn't need the social worker to spend a long time listening to them discuss how difficult it would be and then support them step by step. If therapy is to be empowering, it needs to work from people's strengths rather than to play on their weaknesses. As the therapist pointed out, they had all achieved a great deal.

Finally, the social worker was using a systemic approach: he understood Maria's problem not just in terms of her difficulty or lack of confidence in leaving home, but as a crisis for the family as a whole. Whom would her mother turn to when Maria was gone? Would the arguments between her parents escalate beyond their control? The consequences of change for other members of a client's family might easily be overlooked or ignored by a social worker who works only with individual clients. Change within a system is not a solution to a single problem: for example, removing the symptom or freeing the oppressed. It is certainly possible to empower one member of the system but in such a way that the others are disempowered. In this case the therapist assumed that it was necessary for Maria's parents to change if she was to change. Indeed, he invited them to change first.

In the case of Maria and her family, family therapy seemed to have been empowering. This was confirmed in a follow-up telephone call one year later when all the family members were reported as being well and happy. However, it is important to realise that the process of therapy could have been very different with results which could easily be disempowering.

Responsibility for change
The position that the family members are responsible for change has been criticised. Some have argued that family therapy has over-focused on the family and that historical and sociological influences on families such as poverty, class, gender, age, race and disability have too easily been ignored (Reiger, 1981). Thus families can inappropriately or disproportionately 'take the blame' for behaviours which are caused or strongly influenced by wider social and structural factors: inner city delinquency is one example. At its worst, family therapy can be seen as an instrument of state control, both holding families responsible for creating problems and for caring for its weaker members. Of course, these criticisms have been made of social work as a whole (Donzelot, 1980).

The message of responsibility for change, baldly stated, may not be experienced as empowering in the short term. It is important to remember that empowerment is a process as well as a goal. But some methods of family therapy have rightly been criticised as manipulative and disempowering and some family therapists have undoubtedly taken an authoritarian and highly directive stance. Also, families themselves are not egalitarian institutions and not necessarily empowering of all their members.

Questionable theories and techniques in family therapy
There are a number of different methods of family therapy, not all of which may be empowering. For example, one popular method, developed in Milan, Italy (Selvini Palazzoli, *et al.* 1978) placed such a strong emphasis on the notion of the family as a system that there seemed no room for thinking about its members as individuals: the family was considered as one entity. The consequence of this theorising was that therapy came to be described as a power struggle in which the therapist attempted to outwit the family in the cause of change.

At one point in the development of this approach, great emphasis was placed on the therapist delivering a 'paradoxical' message which contained a 'prescription' (the word used is the same as that for a doctor prescribing medicine). The message spelt out the therapy team's systemic analysis of the family members' interactions, pointing out the 'advantages' of the problematic behaviour or symptom, and prescribed that they should not change. The idea was that the message would have a paradoxical effect with the family rebelling against this advice and thereby changing. Thus, in Maria's case for example, the therapist could have suggested that by staying at home Maria was doing important work for the family, preventing her parents from arguing, her mother from feeling lonely and protecting her father from a heart attack. For the time being, the team might suggest, she should continue with her work.

In many cases, this approach is apparently effective in bringing about change. But, we should ask, is it empowering? Advocates of the Milan method would say that they are always careful to attribute any change to the family rather than to the therapy and argue that the means justify the ends. Indeed, many families are reported as agreeing that changes had nothing to do with the therapy or, if they suspect it had, are unsure how it happened. The problem with this is that families are not empowered: they have learnt little or nothing from the process of therapy and have developed no skills or understanding of how to solve their problems for themselves. If problems recur, they know of few options other than going back to see the therapist, and this they may be reluctant to do.

This method of family therapy contains the most disempowering aspects of family therapy: emotionally detached therapists, technical expertise and a mystification of the process of therapy (Howe, 1989). Some of these features are shared by other methods. For example, both the structural and strategic approaches emphasise a directive approach to therapy and the latter also uses paradoxical techniques. Fortunately, the originators of the Milan approach have since revised their thinking and there has been a general reaction against such methods and indeed against the very assumption that the therapist is an 'expert'. This position itself causes problems, as I will discuss later.

Values
Returning to Maria and her family, it may be noted that the therapist placed con-siderable value on Maria's personal autonomy. An emphasis on individual autonomy and rights within families is, of course, a western position. It is important to recognise that in many other cultures the rights of the individual come second to those of the family group, an ethic which many western therapists find difficult to accept. This example highlights the fact that family therapists inevitably work with a set of beliefs and values about the family, although these are rarely made explicit. Feminist therapists in the United States and Britain have argued that these models of the family, and hence of therapy, have often been blatantly sexist (Goldner, 1985; Perelberg and Miller, 1990).

For example, one way of describing Maria's family would be to say that her mother had become very anxious about and protective of Maria so that a very close relationship had developed between them. This excluded her father and made him jealous so that he reacted angrily. On the basis of this formulation, the therapist might imply that the family 'needed' Maria to stay at home and be dependent on her mother because this would protect her mother from having to have an intimate relationship with her husband. This intervention would almost certainly leave her mother feeling guilty and punished. It tells her, in effect, that she has a problem in her marital relationship for which she alone is responsible. Further, it casts doubt on her motivation for looking after her daughter and implies that she is allowing Maria to suffer in order to meet her own needs. A more disempowering intervention would be hard to imagine.

Feminist critics of family therapy strongly contest the notion that the therapist can somehow be value-free, or 'neutral'. The Milan Approach advocates that therapeutic neutrality is maintained towards different points of view, different members of the system, and even towards the outcome of the therapy itself. The therapist's stance is described instead as being one of 'curiosity' (Cecchin, 1987). However, a neutral position in the face of inequality and injustice is literally without morals. A position of neutrality ignores issues of power in families and ignoring the abuse of power is in effect to condone it. If, for example, Maria's father had been using violence to subjugate his wife and the therapist had ignored it, the message he would have conveyed was that its use was acceptable.

Other critics have argued that therapists can all too easily influence their clients and that the process of therapy can consist in the imposition of the therapist's own value system, and worse. In his book *Against Therapy*, Jeffrey Masson, an American-trained psychoanalyst, subsequently rejected all forms of therapy as an abuse of power. He was particularly critical of family therapy, claiming, 'What is silently apparent in psychotherapy in general is made loudly clear here. The therapist knows best and in family therapy can abandon any pretence of modesty and boldly give orders' (Masson, 1988, p.251).

Family therapists would object that Masson is merely caricaturing the more directive approaches such as structural and strategic family therapy in which typically the therapist sets tasks for the family members to carry out both during and between meetings. In practice, such tasks, involving for example certain members of the family talking or doing things together, will only be carried out if they are carefully explained and negotiated. However, the issue of power is not so easily avoided, particularly because power is exercised through the way in which the therapy relationship is structured.

Thus, for a client to receive a service, he or she has in large measure to accept the therapist's definition of the problem (for example as being a "family problem"), to accommodate to the therapist's particular way of looking at things and to accept his or her way of working (for example by having family meetings). Recently, a number of family therapists, notably Lynn Hoffman, a social worker by profession, have consciously attempted to 'shed' power. Thus therapy has been described as a 'conversation' about a problem between some people who are complaining and some who are not. Therapy in this view is seen as a 'narrative' to which all contribute equally. If therapy is successful, the conversation ends up being one in which no problem is being discussed (Hoffman, 1993).

However, this position seems to ignore the very reasons why families and therapist come to meet each other in the first place. It ignores the very context of therapy, which is inevitably much more than having a "conversation". Simply put, people see therapists either because they want help or because they are required to by judges, psychiatrists, social workers and others who have real power over their lives. It's clearly naïve to talk about the relationship between the therapist and the family as being equal – it's not. Even in the case of a client who pays to see a therapist in private practice, the relationship is based on the client's belief that the therapist's expertise will be valuable in providing some form of guidance. This is surely an appropriate expectation: why else do therapists hang their framed qualifications on the wall of their office? In return, therapists expect recognition, payment and a measure of social power and status. In cases where clients are compulsory attenders for therapy, the power relationship is even more clear cut. To try and pretend that this relationship does not exist is surely dangerous.

It is, in my view, quite appropriate that therapists should lead the therapeutic system. One aspect of the power that a therapist has, by virtue of training, experience and by being an outsider, is the ability to see things in different ways and to help people to find new meanings and new answers. However, therapists must always remember an old social work adage: to start not where they are but where the client is. People will only be open to new ideas if they feel that they have been heard, understood and respected.

It is a truism to say that all of us want to be understood and to understand; to have meaning in our lives But perhaps the most difficult thing is to understand things from another person's point of view. In order to help people understand their relationships with the other members of their family, we need first to understand what they understand about us, what it is like to come to therapy and what they feel about what we are proposing to do. But as professionals we have not been taught to ask these questions, indeed rather the reverse.

Unfortunately there is often a chasm between the expressed intentions of social workers and therapists and their clients' experience of their actions. This chasm is often huge when the therapist has, in addition, the statutory power to control their lives, for example by removing their children or admitting them compulsorily to mental hospital. For these reasons, it is essential that therapy is based on an explicit agreement or 'contract' which sets up a partnership between family and therapist.

A partnership approach to family therapy

The use of contracts in social work has been advocated by a number of writers. The advantage of a contract is, first and most importantly, that it stresses the co-operative nature of the work and the clients' participation, rather than that the expert knows best and will provide a solution. Second, it can help the therapist to maintain a focus in terms of agreed problems, goals and methods of achieving them. If therapy flounders, the therapist and family members can return to the contract and examine the ways in which it is not being met. In some cases, the contract will have to be re-negotiated because different and more pressing problems have emerged or the goals have to be changed. What is important is not that the contract itself is sacrosanct but that there exists an explicit agreement between clients and therapist. Further, there is no 'model' contract and they may be more or less specific.

Contracts can be informal, interim agreements to meet from time to time: for example, to review the progress of a patient suffering from schizophrenia who has been discharged from hospital to his family's care. Alternatively, they can be detailed, written mandatory contracts in the case of child-abusing parents in which the precise requirements on the family members to attend for meetings, and also on the social worker to provide certain services, are spelt out. In these cases, the social worker or therapist with statutory responsibilities must explain her role and duties and include her own goals as part of the contract, including, for example, that a member of the family refrain from violence or stop offending. The consequences of failing to abide by the contract should also be included, consequences which in some circumstances might include returning to court or a child being removed from home. Whilst such outcomes could hardly be said to be empowering, I should argue that being open and direct about the basis for social work involvement in a necessary condition for co-operative work, through which a greater sense of empowerment might be achieved.

Example

Paul, a 25-year-old man, was referred with his parents to a family therapy clinic in a psychiatric unit following his discharge from compulsory detainment in a hospital in another city. He had been diagnosed as '. . . either suffering from a psychotic illness exacerbated by the use of drugs or from a drug-induced psychosis'. His gross delusional behaviour had by this time disappeared.

The first step in contract building is to ask all the family members to describe the problem as they see it and to say what they think is its cause.

Figure 1. First Steps in Contracting and Planning

Figure first appeared in: *Problems and Solutions in Marital and Family Therapy* (1989) Blackwells.

Paul's father was a retired senior personnel officer who defined the problem as his son's lack of motivation. Further, he had a solution: what Paul needed was a demanding job and the route to this was by way of a psychological assessment at a prestigious institute. His mother, on the other hand, thought that her son's apathy was a product of his illness and that he required further psychiatric treatment; in the meantime, she would look after him at home and ensure that he was not 'stressed'. While these statements were being made, Paul indicated his opinion non-verbally by raising his eyebrows, sighing loudly and slouching in his chair. The problem as far as he was concerned was that his parents would not let him lead his own (quiet) life.

The first element in the contract is an agreed definition of the problem: an overarching definition which must necessarily include the different views of the family members. Usually this will be a simple statement of disagreement or worry. In this example, the therapist offered the following statement:

> "After all that's happened, not least Paul's detention in hospital against his will, you're naturally all concerned about his future. But it's clear that you have different ideas about where to go from here. I think it would be useful to discuss these, do you agree?"

Note that the therapist resisted any temptation to diagnose a 'family problem' by highlighting the parent's intrusiveness, the obvious disagreement between the parents about their son, or the latter's contribution to this process through his provocatively immature behaviour. Rather, the therapist stressed the positive aspect, their concern, and tried to find an area of agreement acceptable to all. Note, too, the second part of the statement which proposes a discussion of goals and explicitly asks for their agreement.

At the therapist's suggestion, first Paul's father and then his mother discussed their hopes for Paul with him or, more accurately, they each stated their views in the expectation that he would and should agree with them. As before, Paul indicated his dissent. Once again, the therapist, seeking agreement, proposed an overarching goal:

> "You both want Paul to be responsible and grown-up in his behaviour. Paul wants to take his own decisions and have responsibility for his own life. It seems that there is room for agreement here, is that right?"

This initial goal was limited to Paul; the therapist might have believed that a change in the marital relationship was desirable (he suspected correctly that Paul's parents were having difficulty in adjusting to his father's retirement), but this would remain a matter for later negotiation, when the parents considered that it was a problem for them. The therapist, in other words, started where the clients were: with a concern about Paul's future. He went on to propose having a series of family meetings, taking care to emphasise that this was their choice and that they were free to return to the referring psychiatrist if they preferred. In addition to medication, the options might include individual therapy or possibly attendance at a group for Paul. Since they all said that they would prefer to meet together, at least for the time being, the therapist proposed various details about when, where and how often they should meet and agreed these with all the family members.

Conclusion

Family therapy, with its focus on helping people to resolve their relationship problems and regain control over their lives, can be an empowering method of social work practice. The family therapist aims to establish a positive relationship with all the family members by listening, understanding and conveying an understanding of all their different points of view. The therapist acts as a facilitator, but is also ready to challenge the family member's assumptions and help them think about their problems in new ways. An important ingredient in the approach is to assume that the family members, working together, have the competence to sort out their difficulties. Family therapy works from people's strengths rather than their 'pathology'. The family therapist always uses a systemic approach, understanding problems in terms of their impact on the whole family, and appreciates the consequences of change for each member. The goal is to empower each and every member of the family. On the other hand, some methods of family therapy have more potential for empowering families than others. It is crucial to pay attention to the values of the therapist, the relationship forged with the family and the methods used. An essential element of an empowering approach to family therapy is a clear contract between all parties.

References

Carpenter, J. and Treacher, A. (1989) *Problems and Solutions in Marital and Family Therapy*. Oxford: Blackwell.

Cecchin, G. (1987) Hypothesizing, circularity and neutrality revisited. *Family Process*, 20: 439-447.

Donzelot, J. (1980) *The Policing of Families*. London. Hutchinson.

Fisch, R.; Weakland, J. H. and Segal, L. (1982) *The Tactics of Change*. San Francisco. Jossey Bass.

Goldner, V. (1985) Feminism and family therapy. *Family Process*, 24: 34-47.

Haley, J. (1976) *Problem Solving Therapy*. San Francisco. Jossey Bass.

Hoffman, L. (1993) *Exchanging Voices. A Collaborative Approach to Family Therapy*. London: Karnac.

Howe, D. (1989) *The Consumers' View of Family Therapy*. Aldershot.

Masson, J. (1988) *Against Therapy*. London. Fontana.

Minuchin, S. (1976) *Families and Family Therapy*. London. Tavistock.

Perelberg, R. and Miller, A. (Eds.) (1990) *Gender and Power in Families*. London. Routledge.

Reiger, K. (1981) Family therapy's missing question, why the plight of the modern family? *Journal of Family Therapy*, 3: 293-308.

Selvini Palazzoli, M.; Cecchin, G.; Prata, G. and Boscolo, L. (1978) *Paradox and Counterparadox*. New York. Jason Aronson.

Part IV
Postscript

Some Issues for Social Work Education

Phyllida Parsloe

Although this book is about ways by which social workers can help users to empower themselves, it obviously raises many questions for those who are responsible for educating future generations of social workers. What methods and what kinds of knowledge do students need if they are to develop and assist users along the pathways to empowerment? To begin to answer that question would require at least another book so what follows is a few ideas which arise from the preceding chapters of this book and which other social work educators may want to take forward.

What will have struck any reader of this book is that there is a real dilemma in writing about empowerment. If, as has been argued here, empowerment is a process in which people can be facilitated but never instructed towards empowering themselves, how does one put this in writing? How can we avoid being didactic and prescriptive when what we know has to be done is to allow others to choose not only their own goals but their own route to achieving them. If you have read this far you will know that, to a greater or lesser extent, we have all failed. We have used "ought", "should", and social workers will "need to" because we have still to learn a written language of empowerment. It is, I suspect, more likely to be found in stories or poems which allow the reader the freedom of interpretation, but the academic community has not embraced these forms of communication and to use them leads often at best to confusion and at worst to rejection.

Similar difficulties face the social work educator who wants students to become empowering practitioners. You cannot teach people to be empowering, at least not with any of the usually accepted meanings of the verb "to teach". There is something ludicrous about giving a lecture and arguing for empowering practice when the form of a lecture is one in which the audience is disempowered in order to allow the lecturer to perform. The saying, "the medium is the message" may perhaps help us to consider how social work education can be designed so that the message is not contradicted by the medium. As social scientists, social work educators will be aware that the medium may be a more powerful communicator than is the message.

To empower users it is helpful, although not essential, that students and social workers are themselves empowered. This is not an explicit message in most of the chapters in this book but it is important for social work educators to recognise.

There is, of course, evidence to show that some exceptional people, some of whom are students and some social workers, are able to empower others and raise their consciousness even when they themselves are oppressed by their own educational or employing organisations. But they are rare birds. For the majority of ordinary mortals the adage "do as you would be done by" is apposite. This means that social work educators who want their students to become empowering practitioners may want to ensure that their students feel empowered.

I have written elsewhere in this series about the attempt made in my own university social work department to ensure that the way in which the social work programme was run provided a model which students could use in practice after they qualified, and which empowered them as students (Parsloe 1995). I shall not expand on this here except to say that if social work teachers once begin to address the question of how to create a medium which matches the messages they are giving about the right ways to work with users, they will find, as many other educators seeking to answer similar questions will find, opposition amongst the academic establishment.

Let me turn now to the more specific points which can be drawn out of the preceding chapters.

Kwong Wai Man shows how schools of social work, and particularly their students, can be the carriers for new ideas, skills and methods. They are also of course the purveyors of fashions and, as we know, social work has a tendency to take an uncritical hold of a new idea or method. This is understandable since the ground on which social workers stand is shaky and their need for new directions and certainty great. Nevertheless, it must be the task of social work educators to give these new ideas the kind of critical appraisal which Mr Kwong demonstrates in his chapter. Once an idea has been subjected to such rigorous appraisal, students offer a ready made route into practice. Students in their fieldwork placements and as newly qualified practitioners provide a wide, rapidly flowing channel of communication to change social work practice.

Erika Varsanyi's, Ludmila Harutunian's and Rose Rachman's accounts are actually about the involvement of academic staff and social work students in community development. They illustrate something which I recently observed in South Africa and which may be important for western social work educators to rediscover and that is the reciprocal nature of some kinds of community development. The accounts make clear that the gypsies in Hungary and the women of

Gyumri needed the facilitation, organisation and hope which the social work staff and students could bring. What is also clear is that the staff and students had much to learn from the experiences of the local people. For the students, this was an important contribution to their education, albeit neither the gypsies nor the women of Gyumri were paid as teachers. The staff no doubt also learned a great deal and can use their understanding to produce publications like the chapters in this book. It is perhaps useful to recognise the essential element of reciprocity in this relationship since reciprocity is one important pathway towards empowerment.

Ram Cnaan's chapter opens up an area which is seldom considered by social work educators: the way in which communities can provide the context for people to increase their own feelings of powerfulness and self-esteem. Most social workers spend their professional lives in neighbourhoods where the kind of structures described in this chapter are fragile – if existent at all. What he describes seems to involve large sections of the community, certainly parents and football-age children. No doubt there are equivalent organisations for girls, single people and grandparents. If Dr Cnaan is right in his claim that such organisations are empowering for those who are involved in them, they may offer a model for community workers in less-advantaged neighbourhoods. Social work educators have a tendency to reject the lessons they might learn from the middle classes but to do so may be to deprive other groups in society of access to ways of organising themselves which would provide pathways to empowerment.

Olive Stevenson's and Margaret Boushel's and Elaine Farmer's chapters focus attention upon two key issues in social work education: the attitudes of social workers and the tension between care and protection or control.

These authors are not alone in stressing the need for social workers to achieve attitudes towards users which are conducive to their empowerment. Almost all the writers imply, even if they do not explicitly state, that the attitude of the social worker is crucial. Social workers who aim to help users empower themselves need not only an informed commitment to anti-discriminatory practice but an active commitment to ensuring that users control their own lives to the maximum extent possible. This has proved an easy statement for social workers and their educators to make but a more difficult one to translate into action. Even when they want to do so they may lack the skill to translate values into action, or the approaches towards helping which they have learned from their own society and upbringing make them take control of those who need help.

Social work training offers an opportunity to examine taken-for-granted assumptions and attitudes, to explore values and to learn the skills that allow them to be implemented in action. The statement in the last sentence is carefully phrased since I do not believe it is possible to teach values despite some of the rhetoric to be found in the literature of social work education and of the bodies which validate programmes. We develop our values as we grow, along with our prejudices. Education, if it is of a reflective kind, can help us to make conscious, and explore both our values and our prejudices and such education may lead to a usually gradual change. The most powerful influence upon values which we experience as adults probably comes from our peers. It may therefore be important for social work programmes to ensure that students have the time and the emotional and physical space to talk in small groups of peers. In this way the background which produced the values held by each student is opened up to the backgrounds of others with different experiences which led to different values. A small group of peers can create the kind of setting in which values can be changed since it is usually within relationships that values are formed and can be altered.

The dilemma about this book is that it presupposes that there is an aim for social work which is to help users empower themselves and that certain methods in education and practice are better than others in achieving this aim. At the same time, the very nature of empowerment and the pathways to it is that people make their own choices about their aims and the routes they take towards them. Thus the notion of teaching students appropriate values runs counter to the meaning of empowerment.

Students and social workers face the same problem with users as Audrey Mullender and Jill Reynolds imply. Empowered people may not behave in ways which those who sought to help them to achieve this state would like. The literature of community work has references to neighbourhood or tenants groups or club which, having achieved some hard-won resources or organisation for themselves, then excluded others like them from participation. Empowered people may use their power to exclude or to behave in racist, sexist or ageist ways. How are social workers to respond? The authors here suggest that social workers should state their own position on discrimination and attempt to prevent community groups from, for example, racist comment or action. The kind of empowerment which social work values is empowerment of all and not of particular groups. That message may not be so clear at the start of a route to empowerment than it is later when some power is achieved.

Social work students may need the opportunity to explore these kinds of practice issues and, in order to do so, they need an atmosphere of tolerance. There is a danger in social work education that students are made to feel that certain kinds of views and values are unacceptable and only the so called "politically correct" attitudes can be expressed and shared. Other views and tendencies, such as the prejudices many of us have acquired in our upbringing in a racist, sexist society, are hidden because to express them may expose a student to hostile criticism and even, they may think, to the chance of failure. So social work educators, like social workers with users and community groups, may need to face the question of whether, and if so how and when, they should tolerate intolerance. My own view is that this may be necessary if students are to really be free to examine their own attitudes and, if they wish, to change them. The alternative course runs the risk of turning social work education into an ideological witch hunt. My choice may look like, and may sometimes actually be, the route for moral cowards but it may also allow students to change of their own free will and not have at least change from without imposed on them.

The chapters by Olive Stevenson, Margaret Boushel and Elaine Farmer also highlight another issue for social work education: the question of control as part of social work. Few, if any, students say, when they are interviewed for admission to social work programmes or writing their reason for wanting to be a social worker, that they want to control other people. They are much more likely to state that they want to help others. If "to control" is something they seek, it is unexpressed and may be at an unconscious level. One of the tasks of social work education is to introduce students to the idea that much, if not all, social work entails some aspects of control.

Students may need the chance to consider the nature of control in social work and when it is appropriate. In the United Kingdom, at least, the nature of control is confused because our government seems unable to separate it from punishment. But control and punishment can be different and one major difference arises from their essential nature. To punish means to inflict pain intentionally. The secondary reasons for doing so are many and can include the best interests of the person being punished. To control has no such connection with intentional pain despite the fact that one way of controlling may be by punishment but, like punishment, there are many different reasons for exercising control. In my view, there can be only one reason for social workers exercising control and that is that it is necessary to protect the best interests of the user (or of some other person) when he or she is unable or too young to protect themselves. The writers in this book illustrate this point. They are clear that social workers may need to control some clients when either they or their children need protection. There are circumstances where protection from risk becomes more important than empowerment; when social workers must weigh one value against another and make a choice.

Social work educators will know that discussion of child abuse is an emotive and often painful topic for students but such discussion seems to me to be an essential part of the education of people who will sometimes have to control others. One protection for future clients against arbitrary action by social workers is that in their education they have been able to think through the nature of control in social work and their attitudes to it. It should of course go without saying that the social work curriculum will also include the opportunity for students to learn about and understand the rights which citizens in their country have against coercion by others even when this is exercised in their best interests.

Part III of the book describes some social work methods which can be used to help people to empower themselves. Explicit in John Carpenter's chapter and in mine, and implicit in the other two, is the idea that methods towards empowerment must be chosen with care. Not all social work methods are empowering. Social work programmes may want to encourage students to understand the unspoken messages which lie in the methods they use as well as to acquire expertise in using them. This is a tall order for it involves, as does all social work education, being critical of oneself and one's methods at the same time as one is learning to feel comfortable in a social work role and competent in executing the methods.

This poses another dilemma for social work education. There seems little doubt that the people best able to help others towards empowerment are those who feel they themselves have some power. For social workers, this may be the power that comes from knowledge and professional competence. Social work students come into training to acquire these aspects of power and yet the process of education may, temporarily at least, make them feel they know little and have few skills. The question for social work educators is how to empower students as learners so that they may carry this experience with them as a model for practice.